KONNICHI WA JAPAN

こんにちは日本

Les Omotani

National Textbook Company
NTC a division of *NTC Publishing Group* • Lincolnwood, Illinois USA

Cover photo courtesy of Japan National Tourist Organization.

This edition first published in 1994 by National Textbook Company,
a division of NTC Publishing Group, 4255 West Touhy Avenue,
Lincolnwood (Chicago), Illinois 60646-1975 U.S.A.

Library of Congress Catalog Card Number: 93-84284
Manufactured in Hong Kong.

3 4 5 6 7 8 9 0 WKT 9 8 7 6 5 4 3 2 1

Contents

Foreword

This book is dedicated to the memory of my otoosan, Kumajiro Omotani. He lived a life based upon the values of loyalty, trust, respect and service. It is my hope that all who read this book will be moved to travel the two roads that lead to the discovery of all cultures. As tomorrow's leaders walk more and more in the shoes of their foreign friends the world becomes a better place. Take the risks to journey and meet new people and discover different lands. The future really does belong to those who build the bridges.

I want to express my sincere appreciation to my wife, Lorraine Versteegden, for her continual support, constructive reviews, insightful observations and brilliant perceptions of change. Her unique perspective opened my own eyes to all that was beautiful and noteworthy in Nihon.

I also want to extend my appreciation to all of my friends and colleagues in Canada, the United States and Japan who took the time to forward material, provide interviews, review the manuscript and enhance the development of the instructional design. This book is indeed a product of the collaborative effort that I hope students will experience and value.

Les M. Omotani

About this book

Japan, or *NIHON* (*nee•hon*) as it is called by the Japanese, is a land that has both fascinated and mystified European cultures for over six hundred years. In the fourteenth century the explorer Marco Polo returned from his travels in China with tales of a place he had heard of, a group of islands where there were great riches. He called it *Zipangu*, a name taken from the Chinese words *Jih-pen kuo* which means "land where the sun rises."

It wasn't until 1543, however, when Portuguese sailors arrived on these islands by accident that the first Europeans made contact with the people and the culture of Japan. These sailors called the islands *Japão*, the Portuguese version of *Jih-pen*. From *Japão* comes the English name, Japan.

This book is about other, modern, travellers to *Nihon*. It is the story of Lorraine Kuilboer, a Junior High School student from the United States, who visits *Nihon* with her *OTOOSAN* (*oh•to•sahn* - father) and *OKAASAN* (*oh•kah•sahn* - mother). It is also the story of Lorraine's friend, Kenny Adachi, a *NIHONJIN* (*nee•hon•gin* - Japanese), who acts as Lorraine's *SENSEI* (*sen•say* - teacher) about his country and his culture.

Through Kenny and Lorraine we too are able to travel through *Nihon* and to meet the *Nihonjin* people. In their travels Lorraine and Kenny encounter many different aspects of the culture, old and new. As the title of the book suggests, there are two roads to understanding Japan. It is Lorraine's goal to find out what those two roads are. When you study *Nihon*, this should be your goal too. Like Lorraine, you will learn that *Nihon* is a land that has undergone many changes. As Lorraine learns more about *Nihon*, she also learns more about herself and her own culture. So will you.

While you read this book you will also have the opportunity to learn some *NIHONGO* (*nee•hon•goh* - Japanese language). You have already learned some *TANGO* (*tahn•goh* - words) while reading this page. The first time you encounter *Nihongo* it is written in capital letters and *italics* and is followed by the pronunciation and the meaning, for example *KONNICHI WA* (*kohn•nee•chee•wah* - hello or good day). After that the word appears in italics only. If you wanted to say hello to your teacher you would say: "*Konnichi wa* [teacher's last name] SAN (*sahn* - Sir or Madam, a suffix of respect)." How would you greet your mom or dad? Try saying hello to your neighbor.

Now you are ready to travel the two roads to *Nihon*.

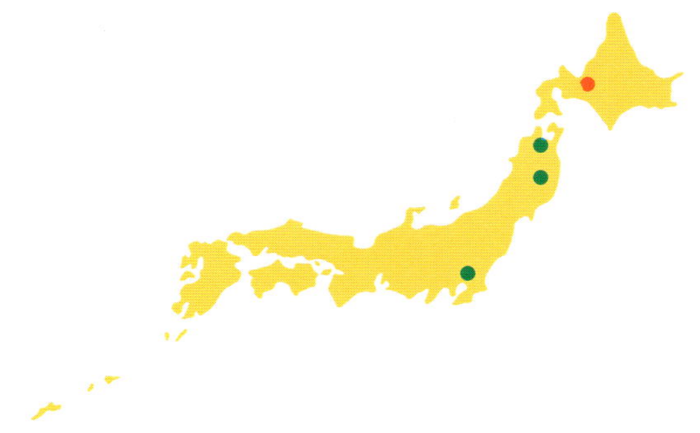

Icon maps are included on the first page of each chapter to help students follow the routes travelled. These icons can be referenced to the larger, detailed map on pages 16-17 of the text.

Green dots indicate the main points en route.
Red dots indicate the destination for that chapter.

Chapter 1

NEIGHBORS AND FRIENDS

JAPANESE VOCABULARY

WORDS

dare	dah•deh	who
doko	doh•koh	where
doshite	doh•shtay	why
Eigo	ay•goh	English
hai	hie	yes
ikaga	ee•kah•gah	how (well are you)
ikura	ee•koo•dah	how much
itsu	ee•tsoo	when
koka	koh•kah	coins
mono	moh•noh	things
nani	nah•nee	what
Nihon	Nee•hon	Japan
Nihongo	Nee•hon•goh	Japanese language
okane	oh•kah•neh	money
satsu	sah•tsoo	bills (as in money) ('o' is added for the polite form)
tango	tahn•goh	words
yen	yen	Japanese money

PHRASES and SENTENCES

Oyasumi nasai	O•yass•oo•mee nass•eye	Goodnight
Sayonara	Say•oh•nah•rah	Good-bye
Sore wa ikura desu ka?	Soh•deh wah ee•koo•dah day•su ka?	How much does this cost?

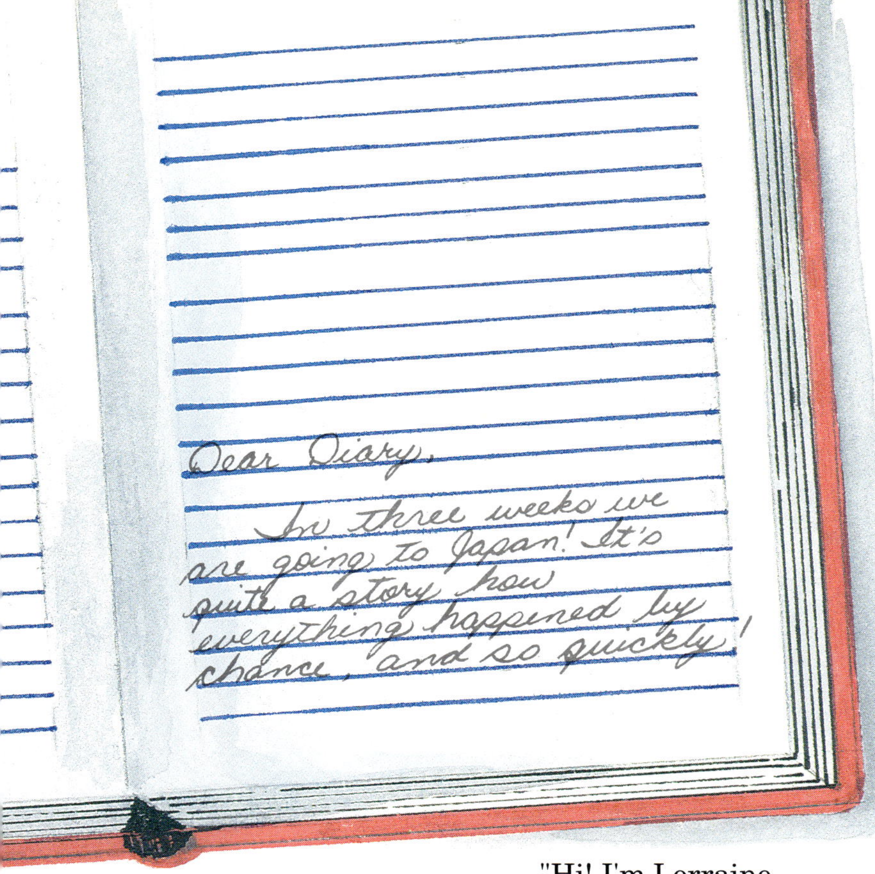

"Hi! I'm Lorraine Kuilboer. Are you moving into the Bruces' house?"

"Hello! I am Kenny Noshiro Adachi," the smiling and good-looking black-haired boy proudly announced. "Yes, we are moving in but this is the house of Adachi, not the Bruces' house. Who are the Bruces?" he asked.

I explained that Karen Bruce was my best friend, but that she had moved away. "I'll sure miss her!" I said. "We were just getting ready to go to junior high school together."

"I'm going to register in Grade Seven at Rocky Mountain Junior High School tomorrow," said Kenny.

"Tomorrow's Saturday!" I exclaimed. "No one will be at the school."

I offered to show Kenny where the school was. Along the way I said, "You sure speak with a strange English accent! Where did you live before coming to Beaver Creek?"

"I once lived in ***Sapporo*** on the island of

Hokkaido, but now our home is in ***Tokyo***, ***Japan***. I have moved to Beaver Creek for this year only. My father's company is investing a lot of money in a new industry here," he continued. "As for my strange accent, I had an English tutor from Cambridge, England, who gave me English lessons every day after school. Before coming here I thought everyone here would speak like I did!" he exclaimed.

"Boy, you sure have a lot to learn!" I said.

"What do you mean?" asked Kenny.

"Well . . . I don't mean to be rude or anything, but your accent and clothes will really make you stick out! It could be rough your first few weeks of school," I explained.

"Oh, I'll buy and wear the school uniform right away! Then I'll look like everyone else!" said Kenny confidently.

I tried not to laugh. I remember saying: "I'm sorry, but except for maybe a T-shirt and blue jeans or the preppy look, there is no uniform. If you want to wear a uniform you'd better join the choir or the soccer team!"

Then Kenny sat, almost fell, down and put his head in his hands. I think he wanted to impress me and be my friend. All he could do was turn red. I think he felt really dumb! After a few moments, I sat beside him and spoke again.

"Listen, Kenny," I said, "we've got a whole week before school starts. I want a new friend and believe me, you could use one right now. If you want, I'll help you to get ready for life at Rocky Mountain Junior High School and Beaver Creek."

Kenny jumped up and hugged me. Then immediately we were both embarrassed. He apologized and I said it was okay. I really did want to be his friend.

The next day, we took the bus downtown. At least Kenny was familiar with **mass transit**. He actually knew quite a lot about North American foods, music, and shows. He told me a great deal about school life in Japan.

After our trip downtown, we sat down to talk about school in Beaver Creek.

"It looks like you are in for some nice changes, Kenny," I said. "You'll have a shorter school week because we have fewer hours each day. And, you don't have to belong to any craft or sports clubs, as you did in Japan."

"I'm not going to miss having school on Saturdays," said Kenny.

"But do the shorter hours mean you get a lot of homework to do before you go home?" he continued. "I'm worried about keeping my marks high enough to get into a good senior high school."

"We get some homework, but after school our time is really our own. You can study as much as you want to, or volunteer for one of the clubs or sports teams like the ones you're used to," I replied.

Kenny did really well at Rocky Mountain Junior High. He was able to help students in his computer class and made some new friends that way. He even scored two goals for our soccer team!

As the months passed, our two families became very close. It was during Easter holidays, when we showed the Adachis the local ski area, that the topic of summer holidays was first mentioned. My dad had been surprised at how well Mr. Adachi could ski.

"There are many ski schools in Japan. Many of our instructors have come to North America to learn how to teach skiing. The dream of most Japanese skiers is to ski in the Rocky Mountains!" said Mr. Adachi.

"I didn't even really think there was snow in Japan," Dad replied.

"Just as we still have a lot to learn about life in the United States, so you probably have much to learn about life in Japan," said Mr. Adachi.

"There's nothing like learning under pressure! " exclaimed Kenny.

I remembered many times during the past several months when he had suffered embarrassing moments. "Kenny, I am sure I would be totally lost if I had to get along in Japan like you've had to here," I said.

"Why not come with us this summer,when we return to Japan, and find out?" asked Kenny. "In fact, because mom and dad have to work anyway, I might be able to travel with you."

Our families quickly agreed that this was an experience they wanted to share together. Mom even forgot that we had been saving for three years for her dream holiday in Hawaii. She only remembered when Dad mentioned that we might be stopping there for a few days on the way home.

Every day after that was filled with planning, excitement and anticipation. We were on the road to Japan. There was so much to do and so much to look forward to.

For example we needed passports and **travellers' checks**. Mr. Adachi also mentioned to Dad that an **international driver's license** would prove helpful.

"How far is it from Japan to Beaver Creek?" I asked.

"Japan, or *NIHON* (Nee•hon - Japan) is 8,240 kilometers from Beaver Creek," said Mr. Adachi as he pointed to the map on the table. "One hundred twenty million people live in an area about the same size as California."

"We'll cross the **International Date Line** from west to east," Mrs. Adachi said.

Kenny looked at his watch. "Its eight o'clock at night here," he said, "which means that it's noon tomorrow in Tokyo."

"It takes about ten hours to fly from ***San Francisco*** to Tokyo," Mr. Adachi said.

I picked up a pencil and did some arithmetic. "If we left San Francisco at nine o'clock in the morning, we'd get to Tokyo at eleven o'clock the next day if we went in the winter and ten o'clock if we went in the summer!" I exclaimed.

"Very good, Lorraine," Dad said with a smile.

WORLD TIME ZONES

The International Date Line is an imaginary line in the Pacific Ocean. All countries have agreed that this line is the place where each calendar day begins and ends.

The world is divided into twenty-four geographic regions called **time zones**. Japan is a long narrow country that all fits into one time zone. There's no daylight-saving time in Japan.

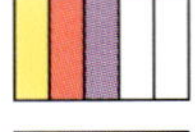
The color of a country or region corresponds to the color of the time zone it belongs to.

Areas where time varies from standard time by half an hour or more are colored gray.

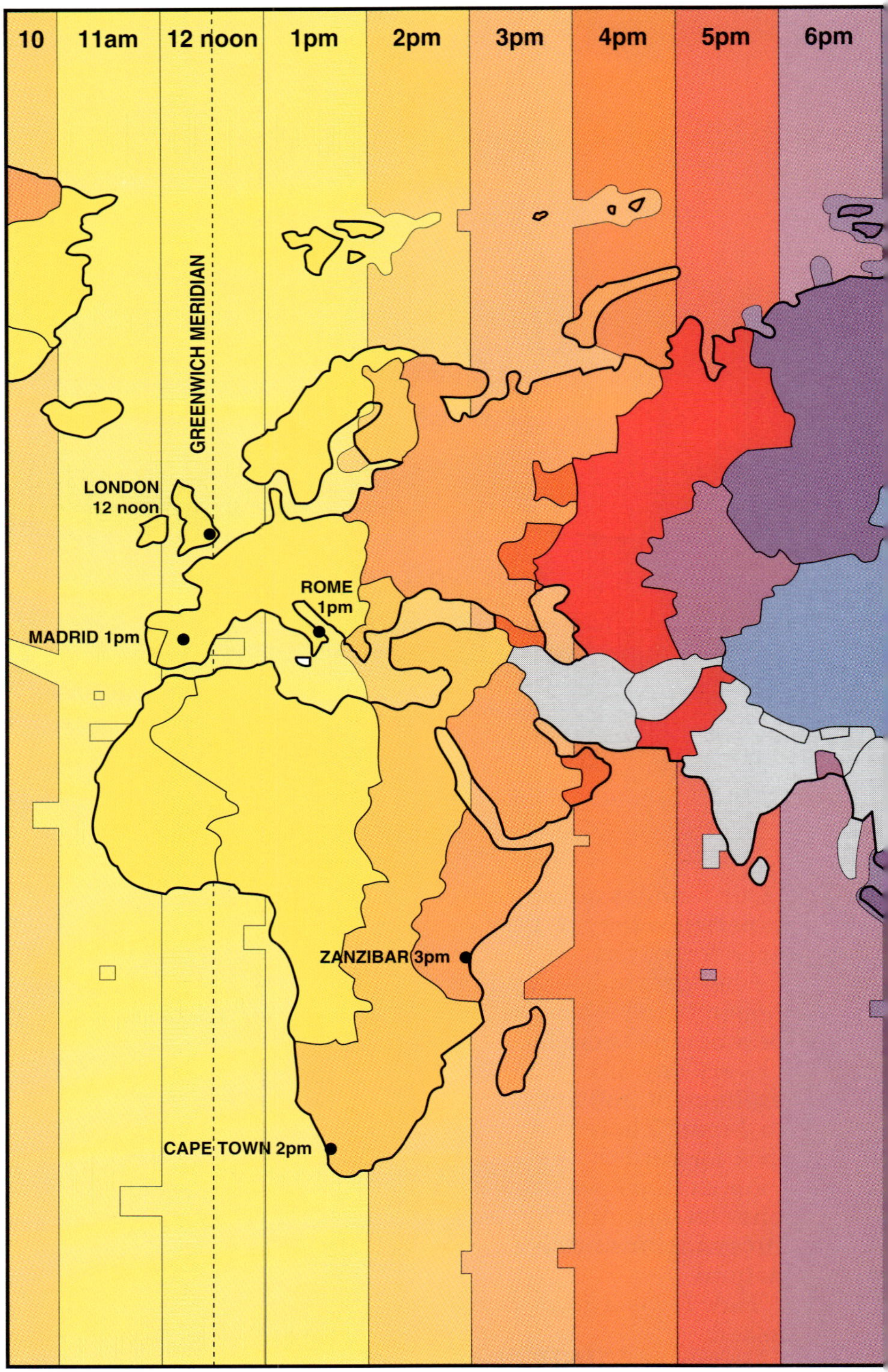

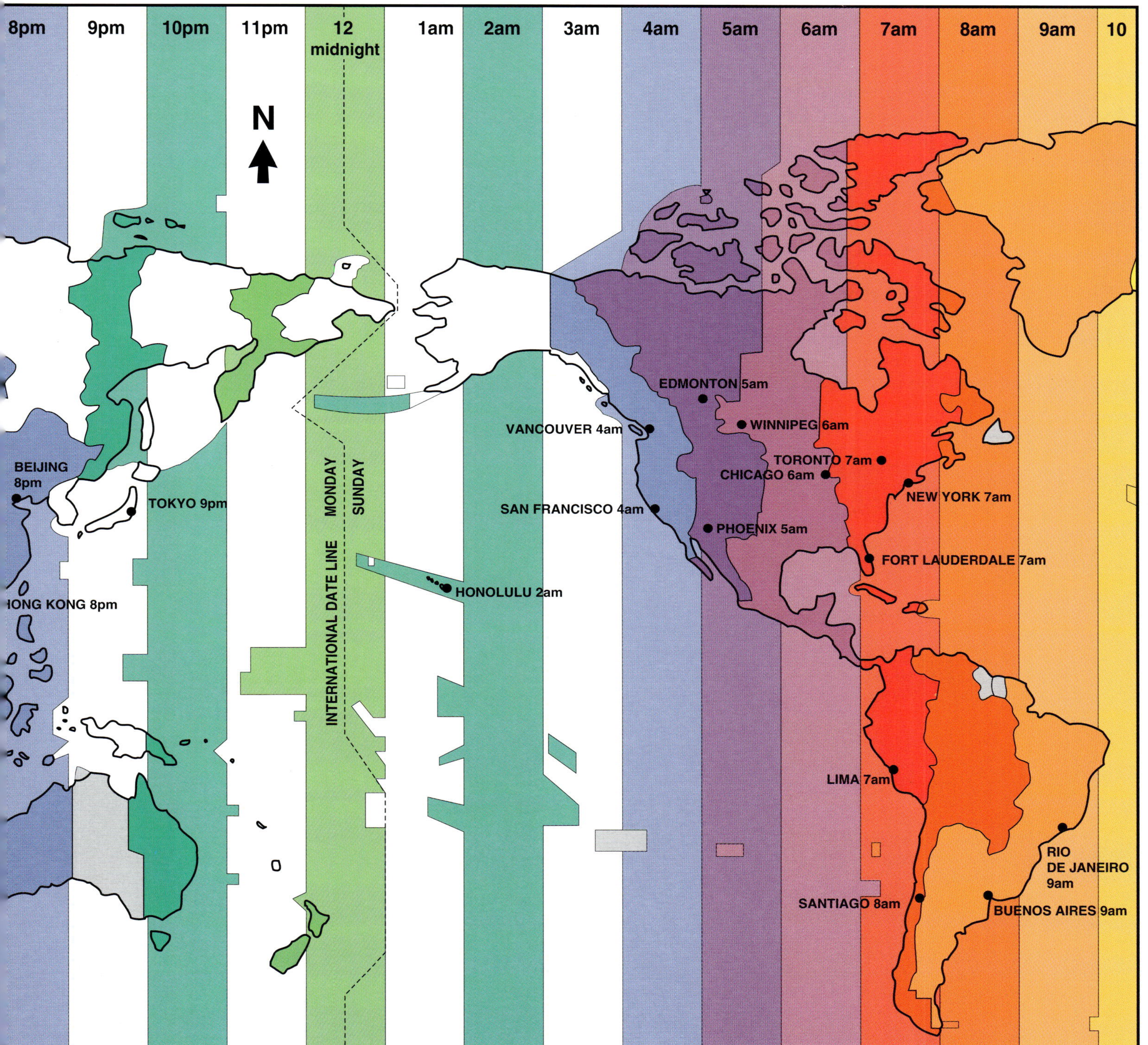
8pm
9pm
10pm
11pm
12 midnight
1am
2am
3am
4am
5am
6am
7am
8am
9am
10
N
MONDAY
SUNDAY
INTERNATIONAL DATE LINE
BEIJING 8pm
TOKYO 9pm
IONG KONG 8pm
HONOLULU 2am
VANCOUVER 4am
SAN FRANCISCO 4am
EDMONTON 5am
WINNIPEG 6am
PHOENIX 5am
CHICAGO 6am
TORONTO 7am
NEW YORK 7am
FORT LAUDERDALE 7am
LIMA 7am
SANTIAGO 8am
RIO DE JANEIRO 9am
BUENOS AIRES 9am

"There's so much I want to know and see," I said. "I've got to get ready before I go! I've got so many questions like what is a dollar worth, how will I order things and—"
"Lorraine!" interrupted Kenny. "Why don't you sit down after school tomorrow and write a list of questions. I'll come over tomorrow evening to help you with your Japanese and try to answer some of your questions. Okay?"
"That would be great!" I replied.
"See you tomorrow."
"Bye! *SAYONARA* !" (*say•oh•nah•rah* - good-bye) I called out, practicing my Japanese.
Right after school the next day I wrote out my list.

What I want to know about Nihon before I go.
Do I need a passport or a visa?
What clothes should I pack?
How much money will I need? Should I take cash or travellers' checks?
Does everyone speak English and Japanese? (NIHONGO)?
What words will I need to learn?
How long will the trip take?
Do I have to sleep on the floor?
What can I buy there?

After I get there
What are the people like?
What is their history?
What are their arts and crafts?
What kind of shopping is there?
How many islands are there?
What are the schools like?
What religions are there in Japan? (NIHON)?
What do they do for fun and recreation?
What industries and businesses are there?
Are their families like ours?
How do they travel from place to place?
Is Nihon a modern or old place?

That evening Kenny helped me. When he saw the list he said: " I can help you with the first part of the list but the second part even has me confused. Maybe I don't know as much about Japan as I thought. It's funny though; many of your questions are the same ones I had before leaving *Nihon* to come to Beaver Creek."
"Did you get all of your questions answered?" I asked.
"I have learned a lot and many of my answers are in files on my computer," answered Kenny. "I know that when I return to *Nihon* my friends will have all kinds of questions about life in Beaver Creek and North America. This way I can be sure to remember everything!"
"I won't be able to take a computer but I could record my answers in my diary, couldn't I?"
"Sure," said Kenny. "You could keep a daily record of what you've learned. When you get home, you can sort the information into separate computer files according to topics like history, food and sports. Now let's talk about some of your questions and begin your *NIHONGO* (*nee•hon•goh* - Japanese) lessons."
"*Nihongo*. What's *Nihongo*?" I asked.
"I told you yesterday that it means Japanese. *Nihon* is Japan and *Nihongo* is Japanese. While we are talking I'll use a *Nihongo* word. If you can understand it then use it! If not, you'll have to ask and I'll explain. That's how you are going to speak *Nihongo*," said Kenny.
"Like a game!"
"Right," replied Kenny. "And then we'll see who has a funny accent."
"Hey! I already said I was sorry," I said in a quiet voice.
"I know but I couldn't resist," answered Kenny. "Now, in *Nihon* many people speak *EIGO* (*ay•goh*- English)."
"*Eigo*? What's that?"
"English," Kenny answered.
"They speak *Nihongo* and *Eigo* in *Nihon*," I repeated.

"Hey! That was really good!" praised Kenny. "Now let's deal with your first question. You'll need a passport but you do not require a visa. We can get a passport application form at the post office," he continued. "It will take about three weeks to get your passport."

"You will need dresses, shorts, sandals, comfortable shoes, a light jacket or raincoat, and an umbrella," said Kenny.

"But I only get to take two suitcases," I complained.

"Not only that," added Kenny, "but the airline also restricts the weight so that we can get off the ground. You must remember that you have to be able to carry your suitcases when we travel from place to place on the trains. The luggage racks only take lightweight suitcases."

"How will I buy things in *Nihon*?" I asked.

"When you want to know the cost of something you ask: *SORE WA IKURA DESU KA*?" (*soh•deh wah ee•koo•dah day•su ka* - How much does this cost?) said Kenny.

Kenny explained that *OKANE* (*oh•kah•neh* - money) is the *YEN* (*yen* - Japanese currency). Their symbol for our $ is ¥. In *Nihon* you need *SATSU* (*sah•tsoo*-bills) and *KOKA* (*koh•kah* - coins) just like here.

"Now let's see *IKURA* (*ee•koo•dah* - how much) some *MONO* (*moh•noh*-things) cost," continued Kenny. "To make a local phone call from a pay phone costs ten *yen* for three minutes or about nine cents. To send an airmail letter costs ¥150 or about $1.50. A movie costs about ¥1500 or about $15.00. Of course, the value of the dollar changes a lot and very quickly. We will check with the bank to see what the current value is just before we leave for *Nihon*," continued Kenny patiently.

"*Sore wa ikura desu ka?*" I said.

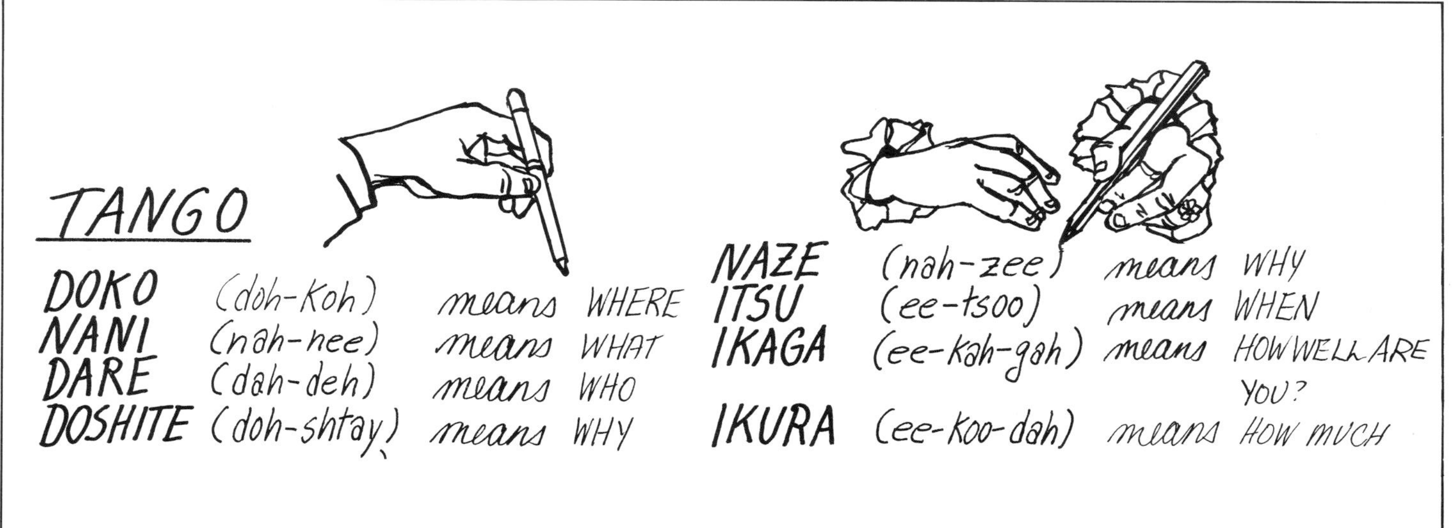

"Good! Keep practicing! You know, there are really only ten or twenty *TANGO* (tahn•goh - words) that you need to know to get by in *Nihon*," reassured Kenny.

"*Tango*," I repeated.

"Here, I'll write the *tango* down on this piece of paper and you can practice the *tango* out loud and then you can write the *tango* on the paper too!" he continued.

"Why do some words mean the same thing, and how do I say hello, good morning, thank you, and stuff like that?" I asked.

"Even in the English language more than one word stands for the same thing," replied Kenny. "We will practice another day. I'll make some flash cards and we will practice using the game," he continued.

"Do you promise?" I asked.

"*HAI!*" (hie - yes) laughed Kenny. "I'll see you tomorrow. *OYASUMI NASAI* (oh•yass•oo•mee nass•eye - good night) or good night!" he said.

"*Oyasumi nasai*." The game was fun. I was really looking forward to travelling to *Nihon*.

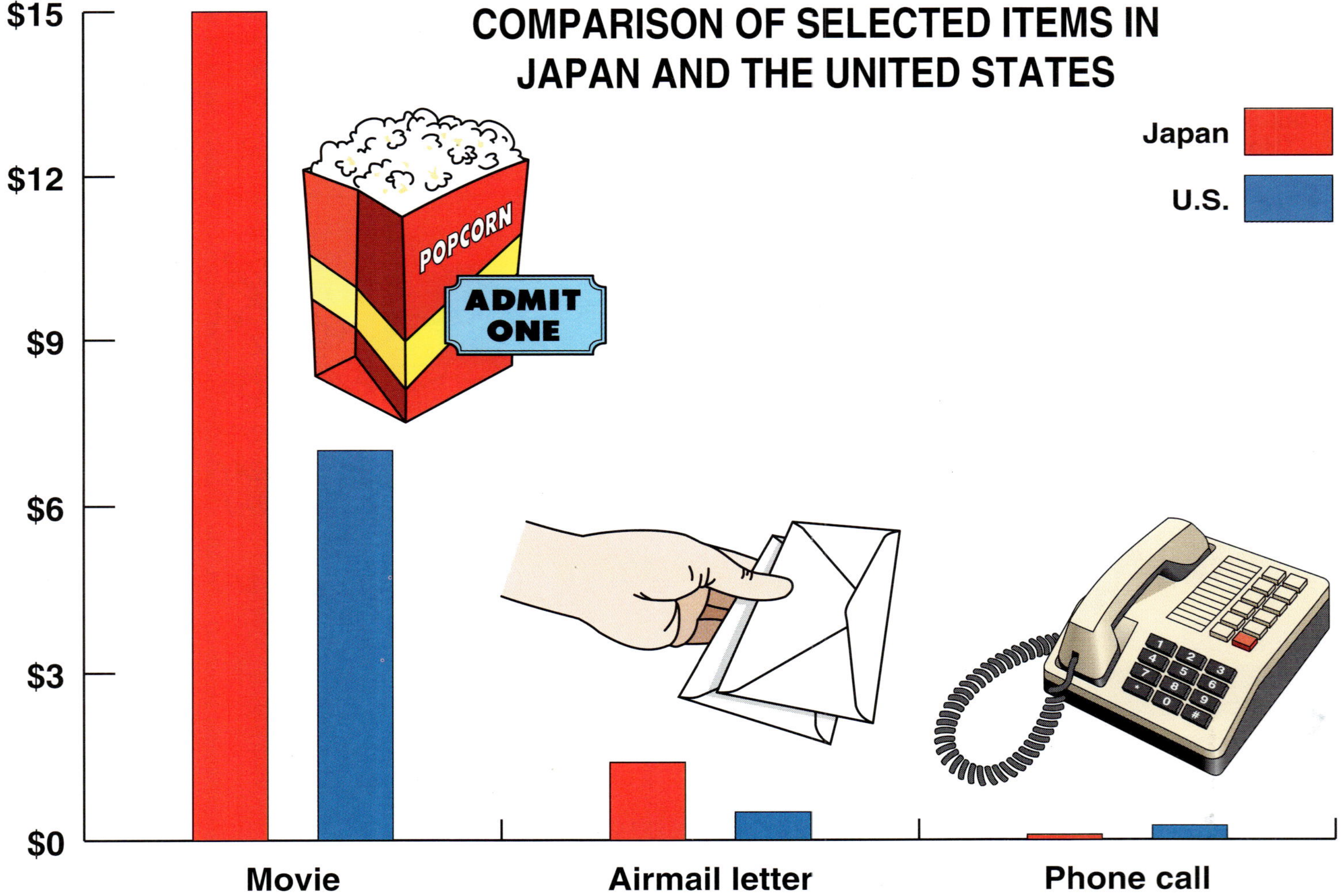

Chapter 2

TWO ROADS TO NIHON

JAPANESE VOCABULARY

WORDS

basu	bah•soo	bus
bento	ben•toe	lacquered lunch box
densha	den•shah	electric train
gohan	go•hahn	steamed rice
Hiragana	heer•ah•gah•na	form of Japanese writing
hashi	hah•she	chopsticks
kanji	kahn•gee	form of Japanese writing
Kanjogaki	Kahn•joh•gah•kee	bill
katakana	ka•ta•ka•na	form of Japanese writing
obaasan	oh•ba•sahn	grandmother
ocha	oh•cha	green tea
okaasan	oh•kah•sahn	mother
Oshogatsu	oh•sho•gat•sue	New Year's Day
otoosan	oh•toh•sahn	father
Nihonjin	Nee•hon•gin	Japanese people
Romaji	roh•ma•gee	Roman letters
shoji	show•jee	door
suimono	su•ee•moh•noh	clear broth
sukiyaki	soo•kee•ah•kee	beef and vegetables
sushi	soo•shee	raw fish with rice
tempura udon	tem•poor•ah oo•don	noodles in broth with deep-fried prawns

PHRASES AND SENTENCES:

Domo arigato	Doh•mo ah•ree•gah•toh	Thank you very much.
Gochisosama	Go•chee•so•some•ah	The meal was very good.
Irasshaimase	Ee•rahsh•shy•mah•seh	Welcome
Konnichi wa	Kohn•nee•chee•wah	Hello/good day
Mata dozo	Mah•tah doh•zoh	Come again.
Nan desu ka?	Nahn•day•su kah?	What is that?
Nani o nomimaska?	Na•neh oh noh•mee•mahs•ka?	What would you like to drink?
Ohayo gozaimasu	Oh•hi•yoh goh•zye•mahss	Good morning

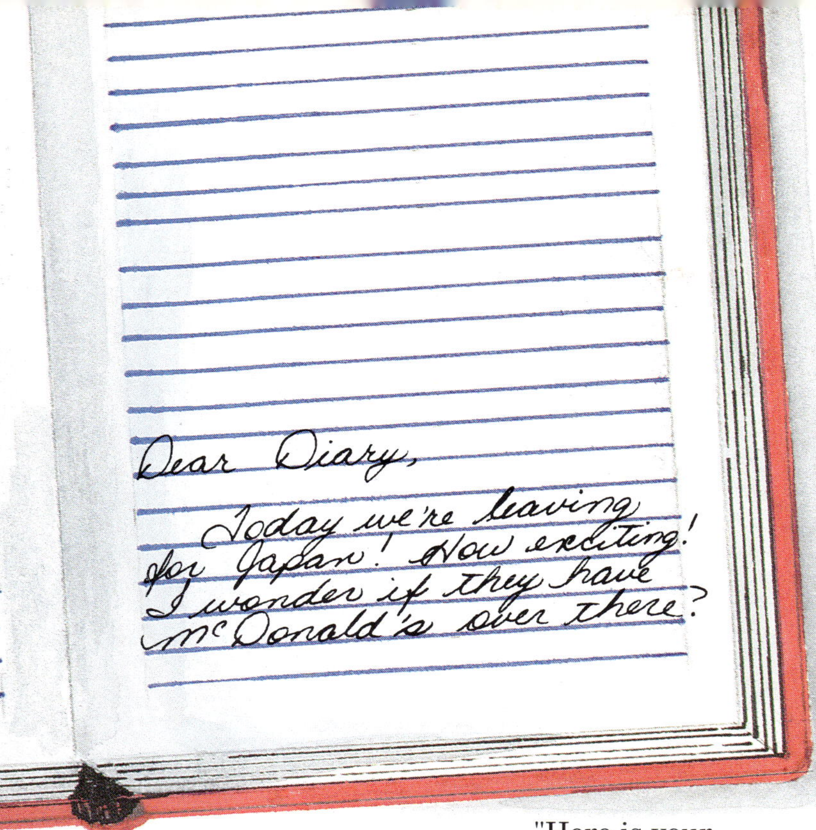

"Here is your **boarding pass**," Dad said. "Now don't lose it."

"Oh Dad! I'm not a kid!" I replied.

"We'd better go to gate twenty-five," Dad said. "It will take a while for all of us to clear security."

"Lorraine!" called Kenny. "Let's get our picture taken in this photo booth. We can keep them as souvenirs."

"Okay," I replied, "but we'll have to hurry. My father wants to go to the boarding area."

We went into the booth, took our pictures, and in a few minutes were looking at them.

"There are so many gates at this intersection, I don't know which is the way to gate twenty-five!" I exclaimed, panic-stricken.

"This is easy. We go to the right," reassured Kenny. "But just wait until you get to the fork in the road in *Nihon* and you have to decide which way to go!"

"I don't understand," I replied.

"There are always two roads or choices in *Nihon,* the old or traditional and the new or modern. Some people get lost in between. Don't worry. You will see what I am talking about when we get there," he continued.

"You know, Kenny, I didn't realize that there would be so many *NIHONJIN* (*Nee•hon•gin* - Japanese people) on this plane to *Nihon*," I said, continuing to play our Japanese language game.

"Japanese travel to all parts of the world, especially North America. Many of the passengers on this plane have been holidaying at Yosemite National Park. There are also many Japanese-Americans who are going to visit *Nihon* on holidays or business. Although they look Japanese, many were born in the United States and may speak the language only as well as you," replied Kenny.

"That would be something! At least most people will know that I cannot speak *Nihongo* very well. But I'm sure that if you look Japanese, even if you were born in the United States, they would expect you to speak *Nihongo*. It still seems weird that there are only twelve or so people on this flight that are not of *Nihonjin* **ancestry**," I continued quietly. "It's interesting and exciting to hear the captain and the flight crew speak in *Eigo* and *Nihongo*."

"Lorraine, look at those two girls across the aisle! I'll bet they are going to Japan to be models!" exclaimed Kenny as he stared in their direction.

JAPANESE WRITING

Katakana are used to spell foreign words and names. Many signs in Japan are also written in *ROMAJI* (*ro•ma•gee* - roman letters).

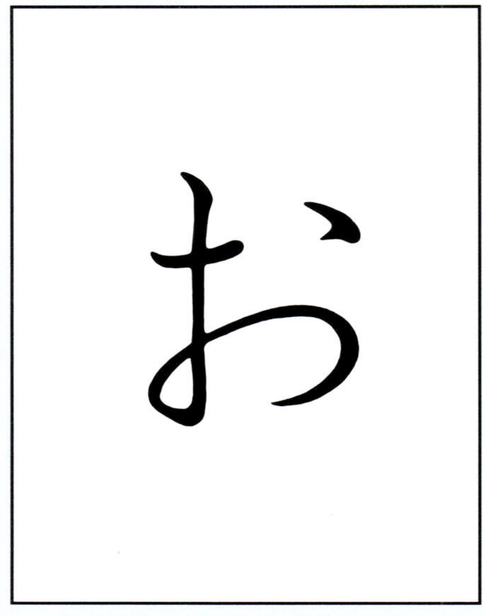

Hiragana symbols are used to spell out words of Japanese origin.

Kanji characters or symbols represent whole words or ideas. *Kanji* symbols are square in appearance.

"How do you know that?" I asked.

"Well, first they are both tall and slim, and good-looking!" Kenny said with a chuckle.

"Kenny, that's a **sexist** judgement!" I responded, not sure whether Kenny was serious or not.

"Let me finish!" Kenny protested. "They also have photo albums and portfolios. I saw the girl with the brown hair show the blond-haired girl her pictures. The boy sitting next to them in the leather outfit may also be a fashion model."

"Why would the *Nihonjin* want models from North America?" I asked.

"You just wait until you see *Nihon* and have people stare at you and ask for your picture and you will have your answer. In *Nihon* Japanese clothes are modelled by Japanese models, but fashions from Canada, the United States and Europe are usually modelled by foreign models. This is even true for mannequins," replied Kenny.

I daydreamed about being a model in *Nihon* until the flight steward handed us some forms.

"*NAN DESU KA*?" (*nahn day•su kah* - what is that) I asked.

"These are departure and arrival forms," the steward said. "Give your passport numbers, home address, nationality and purpose of your trip."

The flight attendants gave us some Japanese magazines to look at. Kenny explained that the Japanese writing system derived from the Chinese. Some of the words in the magazines were written in *KANJI* (*kahn•gee* - form of Japanese writing) where each character or symbol represents a whole word. He also pointed to *HIRAGANA* (*heer•ah•gah•na* - form of Japanese writing) and *KATAKANA* (*ka•ta•ka•na* - form of Japanese writing) symbols that stand for individual letters or syllables.

I told Mom that I couldn't wait to get to Tokyo to go to the famous shopping area called ***Ginza***.

Mr. Adachi said that he was sorry to put a cloud on my excitement to shop in the famous area of Tokyo, but we had several things to do at ***Narita Airport*** even before we took the one-and-a-half-hour bus trip to ***Tokyo City Air Terminal*** in the city.

I was still too excited to be disappointed.

Kenny pointed out a number of Japanese men who had left their seats and had gathered together. One man opened a *BENTO* (*ben•toe* - lunch box) and passed it around to his friends. The box was like a lunch box except it was made of lacquered wood and contained rice balls, slices of meat and fish, and cakes.

The flight crew offered us a choice of fish or chicken for a meal. Kenny and I both chose chicken. We were also offered a choice of knives and forks or *HASHI* (*hah•she*-chopsticks). I decided to practice eating with *hashi*. The chicken was cut into pieces. Kenny said that in *Nihon*, large pieces of meat are often pre-cut to avoid embarrassing situations and problems.

I did really well with my *hashi*.

"You're getting pretty good with your *hashi* but I bet you can't pick up your tiny tomato – like this!" Kenny said, holding up his cherry tomato with his.

"You're on!" I said, and I did it!

Then I had a question that even Mr. Adachi could not answer: "How do you butter a bun with chopsticks?"

The pilot told us to get ready for landing. I looked out the window but all I saw was the Pacific Ocean. Then suddenly, there it was! The "Land of the Rising Sun," *Nihon* – Japan! I felt the wheels touch down and saw rows of shrubs and trees

lining the far runway – it was like we were landing in a huge garden.

I saw a sign made of flowers and shrubs that said Narita International Airport. It was a very busy airport. I had never seen so many planes in one place before. There were planes from all over the world.

As we cleared **customs**, the customs agent said: "*OHAYO GOZAIMASU!*" (*oh•hi•yoh goh•zye•mahss* - good morning).

"*KONNICHI WA*," (*kohn•nee•chee wah* - hello, or good day) I replied.

I was surprised when the agent said: "Very good! You speak *Nihongo* very well!"

"Thank you," I answered. "And you speak *Eigo* very well!"

At the Japan Railways counter, Dad exchanged our Japan Rail **vouchers** for passes. The ticket agent, Mr. Adachi and Dad were busy looking at a map and pages of train schedules. The agent understood *Eigo* very well.

Dad tried to explain most of our plans. Mr. Adachi must have felt things were going well because he went to buy a newspaper and left Dad to make the reservations.

"Travelling on your own is the only way to discover the real *Nihon*!" I heard Mr. Adachi say as he walked away.

Our travel plan would take us from Tokyo to ***Morioka***, ***Aomori*** by *DENSHA* (*den•shah* - electric train). The ticket agent showed us that we could go from Tokyo to Aomori on a super-express train nicknamed the **bullet train**. However, we would have to take a ferry across the ***Tsugaru Straits*** from Aomori to ***Hakodate***. Then we would join the bullet train at Hakodate for our trip to Sapporo.

"You can stop inland at Morioka going and ***Sendai***, on the coast, coming back," the ticket agent said. "That way you can see different regions of *Nihon* and enjoy the four-hour ferry ride in the daytime."

"From Sendai on your return you will pass through Tokyo, ***Kyoto***, ***Hiroshima***, and ***Osaka*** ."

The ticket agent began preparing our reservation cards. Kenny explained to me that the green slips of paper are reservation cards. "They are like tickets. They have the track number, place and time of departure, place and time of arrival, car number, seat number, and the name of the train. We can change our reservations at any time at a local Japan Rail station if we change our travel plans."

"I'm so glad that we can make all of our travel arrangements right here with this one stop!" Mom exclaimed.

I was too busy watching all the people to reply. Dad and the ticket agent finished the last computer printed ticket from Osaka to Tokyo and the agent reviewed the departure place and arrival place of each ticket. I offered to write the name of each place in *Eigo* on the ticket because everything was written in *katakana*. Everyone agreed that this was an excellent idea! I was really proud!

The agent gave us all of the maps and schedules that he had been using. He made a low bow and thanked us for allowing him to serve us. I felt funny! Here was a man who had spent so much

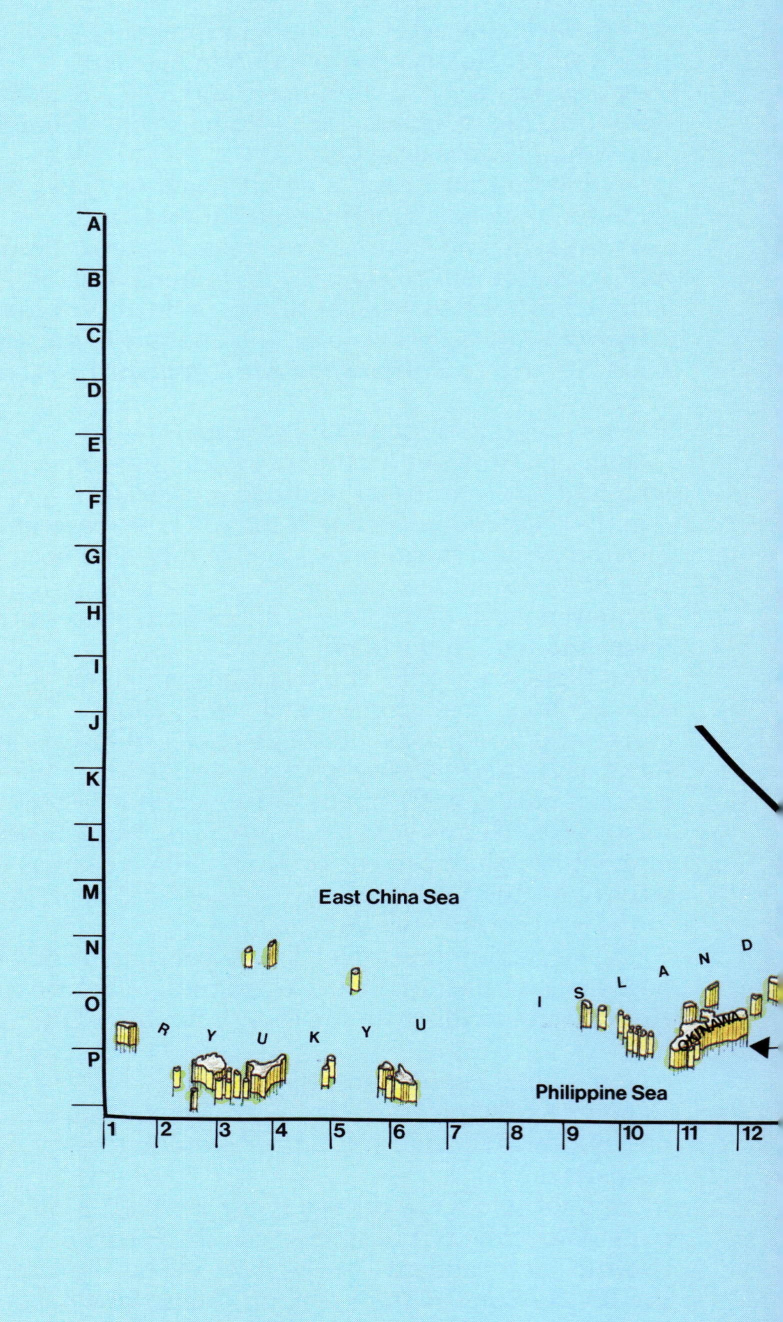

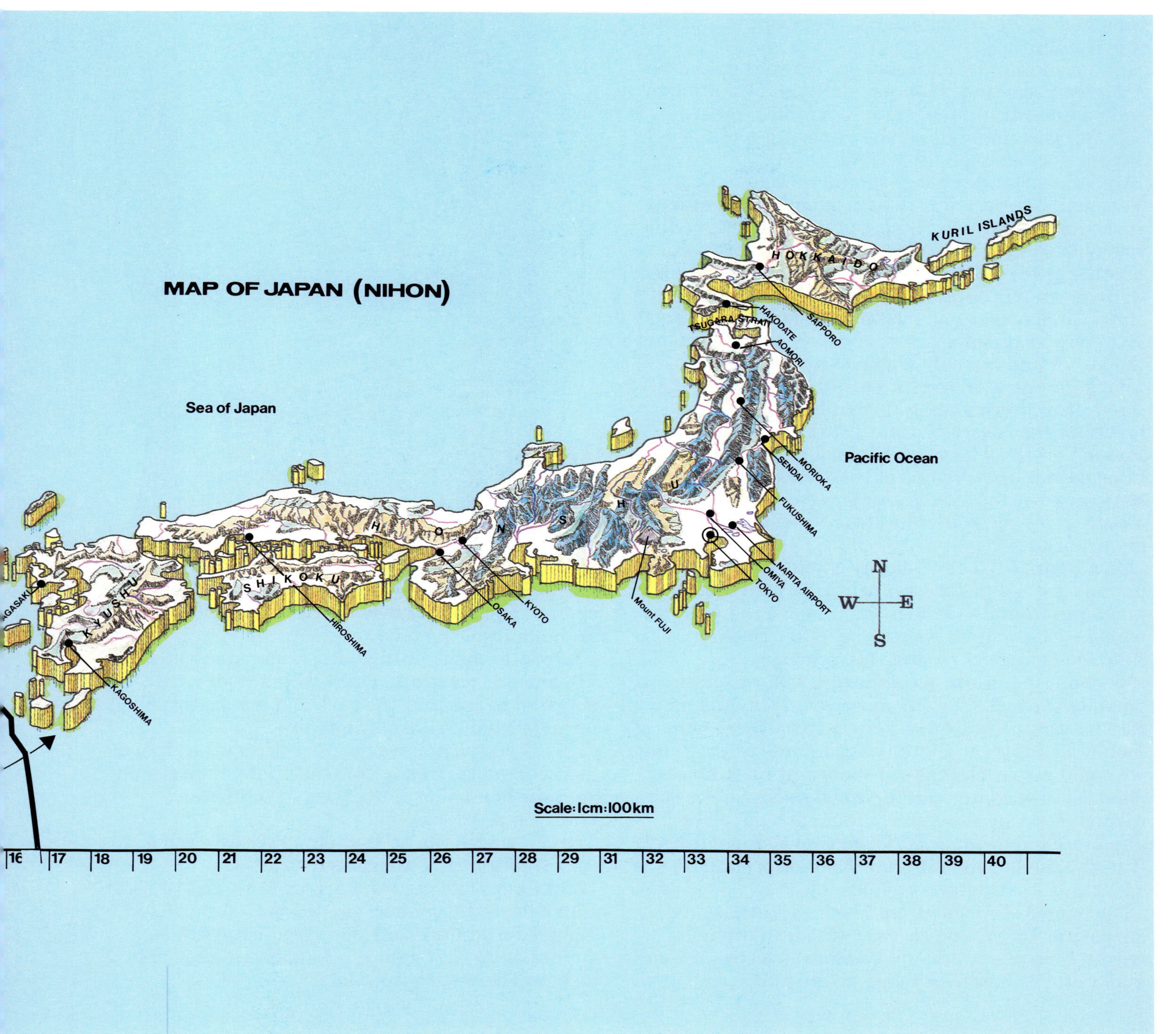

MAP OF JAPAN (NIHON)
Sea of Japan
Pacific Ocean
KURIL ISLANDS
HOKKAIDO
SAPPORO
HAKODATE
TSUGARA STRAIT
AOMORI
MORIOKA
SENDAI
FUKUSHIMA
HONSHU
NARITA AIRPORT
OMIYA
TOKYO
Mount FUJI
KYOTO
OSAKA
HIROSHIMA
SHIKOKU
KYUSHU
KAGOSHIMA
N
W
E
S
Scale: 1cm: 100km
16
17
18
19
20
21
22
23
24
25
26
27
28
29
31
32
33
34
35
36
37
38
39
40

time and effort to make our arrangements and he was thanking us!

I reached into my backpack and gave the man an American coin and a Liberty Bell pin. Mrs. Adachi smiled and Mr. Adachi said: "Lorraine, you are beginning to understand the importance of the Japanese custom of gift giving!"

Mr. Adachi said that we should now go to the National Tourist Office. The woman at this office spoke and understood both *Eigo* and *Nihongo*. She was able to say one sentence to Mom in *Eigo* and another to Mrs. Adachi in *Nihongo*. She offered to write down our hotel names and addresses using *kanji*. "If you ever need assistance finding your way just show this paper to a taxi driver or a person on the street and he will be able to help you!"

We found a lot of brochures and maps for each of the areas we were going to visit as well as a brochure that described the Tourist Information Phone Service**.** There were lots of pictures and information in every one of these brochures. I took some just because the pictures were so nice. I made a note in my mind to take some to school to show my art teacher.

Once again I felt that simply saying thank you was not enough. I quickly found an American coin and a pin from Beaver Creek and gave them to the woman. She smiled, bowed and said: "*DOMO ARIGATO*." (*doh•mo ah•ree•gah•toh* - thank you very much).

We went to a **money exchange** teller to trade our travellers' checks for Japanese *yen*. Mrs. Adachi told me that it was quite safe to carry large sums of money in Japan as there is little crime or theft, but we could also exchange our money at most hotels. All exchange centers are licensed and give the rate quoted or set by the government each day. The Japanese paper *satsu* all looked very much alike. I was not used to the different *koka*, especially the ¥500 coin worth almost $5.00.

The express freeway from Narita International Airport to Tokyo City is a very modern highway with toll booths in several sections, overpasses, and elaborate bridges over many rivers and

canals. The sides of the road often have high concrete and metal noise barriers to shelter the residents from the noise of the traffic.

The center aisle, or divider, is often decorated with shrubs, trees and vines. I was really surprised to see that the cars and trucks travelled on the left hand side of the road.

"This is something we borrowed from the British. I was very surprised to find out that you drove on the right hand side of the road in the United States," Mr. Adachi said.

"Yeah," said Kenny, "Dad almost drove into a truck the first time we rented a car."

"And I kept looking for a driver to sit on the right hand side of the vehicle!" added Mrs. Adachi.

I played a game with Kenny, counting the number of large freight trucks passing each side of the bus. There sure were lots.

Japanese satsu and koka.

The sides of the roads were like flower beds. I saw my first **rice paddies**. Mr. Adachi explained that they were being irrigated with water and were very green while growing, but like wheat, would turn a golden yellow when ready to be harvested. In some parts of southern *Nihon* there is an early spring harvest as well as the traditional fall harvest.

I asked Mrs. Adachi why the *Nihonjin* had their laundry hanging out of the windows and balconies of the apartments and condominiums. She explained that most families did not like to use up the space and money on an electric dryer. They also liked the smell of clothes dried in the open air.

"All but these people," Kenny said. "Look, they are on the twelfth floor and this bus is blowing its exhaust right in their apartment windows!"

It was the first time that I noticed all of the traffic crossing underneath us and how high up we were. At some points the expressway we travelled on was several stories high.

"The *Nihonjin* have adopted many of the latest electrical appliances, but there are some things that they still prefer to do the old ways simply because of **tradition**," Mrs Adachi added. "Many of the women who do not work outside of the home take a great deal of pride in the quality of their homemaking services, including doing the laundry."

I made a note in my mind to ask Mrs. Adachi more about the role of women in *Nihon*.

Mr. Adachi was pointing to a building beside a very tall skyscraper. It was only two stories high and had a sloping and curved roof. He said that the building was an older house built according to the Chinese architectural style. Most of the modern skyscrapers were stark, multi-sided, very tall and had lots of concrete and glass.

We passed several large industrial plants and factories. A lot of construction activity existed everywhere I looked. Before I knew it we had arrived at the Tokyo City Air Terminal.

As we went to claim our luggage, we passed rows and rows of limousine buses. I asked Kenny where the planes were. He laughed: "This is an arrival and departure center for people who want to go from Tokyo to Narita International Airport. This is a *BASU* (*bah-soo* - bus) station."

A group of *Nihonjin* were just getting their luggage. "Oh look, pineapples from Hawaii!" Mom said.

"Remember, Goro and Ted, next Christmas we get to go to Hawaii for a reunion!" Mrs. Adachi added.

Japanese cities are large with many modern buildings.

"But Fumiko," Mr. Adachi laughed, "your mother will never let us miss two New Year's celebrations in a row. You know how important the celebration of New Year's is to the older people."

"New Year's Day, or *OSHOGATSU* (*oh•sho•gat•sue* - New Year's Day) is the most important holiday in *Nihon*," Kenny explained. "Almost all the shops and factories close for three days. It's a time for people to be with their families and the trains are full of people going home. The New Year's season is about two weeks long."

"Just like Christmas," I said.

"Yes," said Mrs. Adachi. "There are some similarities. We send *Oshogatsu* cards which are like Christmas cards. The celebration is important because it symbolizes a time of renewal."

Mr. Adachi and Dad were helping one man who had brought boxes of pineapples and macadamia nut chocolates. Kenny said that the man was embarrassed by all of the luggage and gifts but that he had many relatives who loved chocolate! There it was again, the importance of gift giving!

When we had our bags we gave a man the claim check stubs and went through automatic sliding doors with him. Kenny said he likes to call them "electric" *SHOJI* (*show•gee* - door).

The man took us to some waiting taxis. Both this man and the taxi drivers wore white gloves. I got a surprise when the back door of the taxi opened automatically. Mr. Adachi reminded me not to close the door because the driver controls it from his seat.

The taxi driver spoke very little *Eigo* and could not understand Dad. Mr. Adachi laughed and spoke to the man in *Nihongo.* We arrived at our hotel after a short drive.

Inside the hotel, everyone was dressed in uniform and was very friendly and polite. The women at the registration desk were most helpful. Both of them spoke *Eigo*.

The Adachis helped us take our things to our rooms. Kenny and Dad were going to stay in one room and Mom and I in another.

The hotel was very clean and neat but everything seemed small. It really seemed very small when all six of us met in Dad and Kenny's room.

"Now you know why the *Nihonjin* spend a lot of time dining and entertaining outside of their homes," Mr Adachi said. "Many apartments are no bigger than this. Our house is larger but still it would be crowded for the seven of us!"

"Seven?" I asked.

"Oh yes!" Mr. Adachi said. "You may have forgotten but Kenny's *OBAASAN* (*oh•ba•sahn*- grandmother), my *OKAASAN* (*oh•kah•sahn* - mother), lives with us. She has been taking care of our house this past year. Since my *OTOOSAN* (*oh•toh•sahn* - father) died in the Second World War, it has been my responsibility as the eldest son to take care of her. We will have you to the house for supper before you leave Tokyo and head for Hokkaido," he continued.

"Well, Goro and I must be going! We have to get ready to rejoin the working people in *Nihon* once more!" Mrs. Adachi announced.

"Yes, Fumiko, now you have to get used to obaasan telling you what to do!" laughed Mr. Adachi.

"In *Nihon* kids and the elderly get lots of respect and attention. Some *okaasans* don't feel that their sons' wives are ever good enough for them," Kenny whispered.

"Kenny, you be good!" warned Mrs. Adachi. "Remember you're never so far away that the Kuilboers can't send you home!"

"I'll be better than good! I'll be great!" yelled Kenny.

"Alice, there's a good restaurant two blocks down the street towards the subway station," said Mrs. Adachi. "We will contact you after dinner to arrange our plans."

"*Sayonara*," replied the four of us together. I was very tired and very happy. We were finally on the road to discovering *Nihon*!

After we finished unpacking we went to the restaurant Mrs. Adachi recommended. At the entrance to the restaurant there were fifteen to twenty plastic models of various meals, dishes, desserts, and drinks that we could order once inside. The models were very realistic. When we stepped on the welcome mat the *shoji* slid open and we entered to a loud greeting from all of the staff: "*IRASSHAIMASE!*" (*ee•rahsh•shy•mah•seh* - welcome).

The waitress brought us each a hot towel to wipe our hands and face with. Then we pointed to the model we wanted for our meal. Everyone began with *SUIMONO* (*su•ee•moh•noh* - clear broth soup). Mom had *TEMPURA UDON* (tem•poor•ah oo•dun - noodles in broth with deep fried prawns) and Dad had *SUSHI* (*soo•shee* - raw fish and rice). Kenny and I ordered *SUKIYAKI* (*soo•kee•ah•kee* - beef and vegetables in a sauce). Everyone except Dad was given a side bowl of *GOHAN* (*go•hahn* - steamed rice). The waitress asked us: "*NANI O NOMIMASKA*?" (*na•neh oh noh•mee•mahs•ka* - What would you like to drink?)

We all decided to have *OCHA* (*oh•cha* - green tea). The meal was delicious. Everything tasted fresh and light. I remember thinking how beautiful each

Changes in Japanese Eating Habits

Food groups	Average (1934-38)	1970	1982
Cereals	71.8%	49.9%	42.2%
Potatoes and root starches	6.2%	4.5%	6.3%
Pulses (Miso and Shoya)	7.2%	6.9%	5.7%
Vegetables and fruits	3.3%	5.1%	5.1%
Animal foods	1.4%	9.0%	12.2%
Fish and shellfish	1.6%	4.0%	4.9%
Sugar	7.4%	11.2%	9.1%
Oils and Fats	1.1%	9.4%	14.5%
Total	100%	100%	100%

Source: Food Balance Sheet, Japanese Ministry of Agriculture, 1984

A variety of Japanese dishes.

dish was. They all had lovely designs painted on them in blue and white.

Mom and Kenny talked about the plates and pictures on the wall. There were Delft Blue plates from Holland and paintings by European artists. Kenny explained that the Japanese have appreciated the fine works of other cultures for a long time. "In school we learn a lot about what has been borrowed from other cultures," he said.

We paid our *KANJOGAKI* (*kahn•joh•gah•kee* - bill) and Kenny said: "*GOCHISOSAMA*" (*go•chee•so•some•ah* - the meal was very good) to the waitress.

The waitress replied: "*Domo Arigato. MATA DOZO*" (*mah•tah doh•zoh* - come again).

As we were leaving the staff again called out "*Oyasumi nasai*!"

We responded with our own "*Oyasumi nasai*!"

On the walk back to our hotel we didn't talk very much. I think we were all just trying to absorb all of the day's experiences.

We went to bed tired! My last thoughts were of the downtown rush hour, the maze of people, the unreadable signs, the bicycles, the taxis, the delicious food and the friendly people.

We would indeed have many choices to make as to what road we would take to understand the culture of *Nihon*. I couldn't wait for tomorrow!

Chapter 3

TRAVELLING THE HIBIYA LINE

JAPANESE VOCABULARY

WORDS

geisha	gee•shah	Japanese lady artist/ performer
kimono	kee•mo•noh	elaborate coat/dress
mochi	mo•chee	Japanese pastry
udon	oo•dohn	noodle dish
yukata	yuh•kah•tah	Japanese dress

PHRASES and SENTENCES:

Ichiban!	Ee•chee•bohn!	Number one!

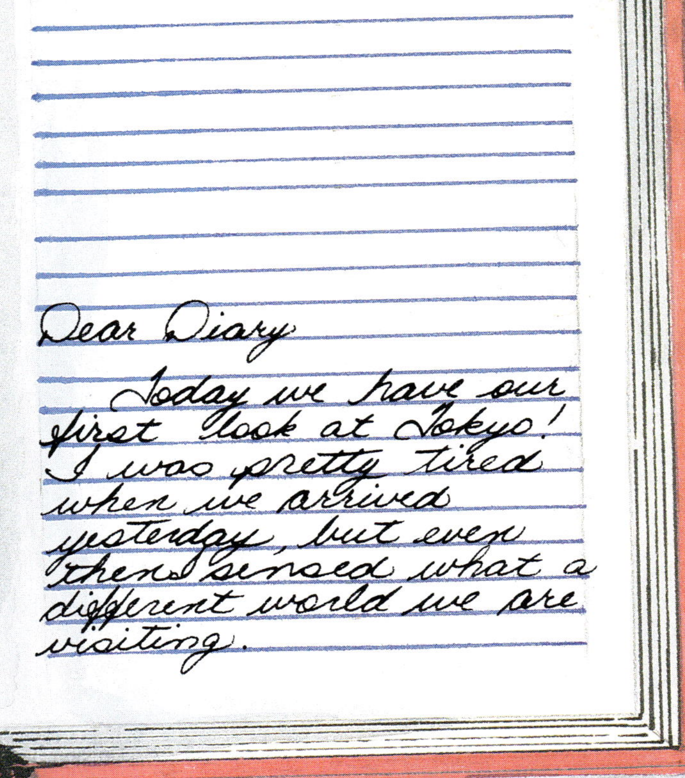

We figured out that the closest subway was ***Kodenmacho***. We went to a travel bureau in our neighborhood and made arrangements for a tour of the **Imperial Palace**. Dad spoke to a lady who understood *Eigo* and made the reservations.

We went to Kodenmacho Station to take the subway to ***Ueno***. Kenny showed us the automatic ticket vending machines. We each put in *koka* worth ¥120 and received a small green ticket, which was then punched by a man at the entrance gate.

"Make sure you keep your ticket stub. You have to hand it in at the other end. In *Nihon* all transportation runs on a user pay basis. You pay for how far you are going," Kenny told us.

We looked at our subway map and saw that the next stop was ***Akihabara Station*** and then Ueno Station. I pointed out that there were three circles on the platform and on signs by the tracks every ten to fifteen meters.

"I'll bet that's where the doors stop!" I stood right on the circles and sure enough when the subway train arrived at the station I was standing right in front of an open door.

The trains are very prompt and fast. Kenny boasted that you could set your digital watch by the railway time and travel throughout *Nihon* without ever having to reset your watch. We had less than sixty seconds to get on and find a seat.

"Today we are lucky," said Kenny. "Often we would all have to stand like those men over there and hold onto the overhead straps for balance."

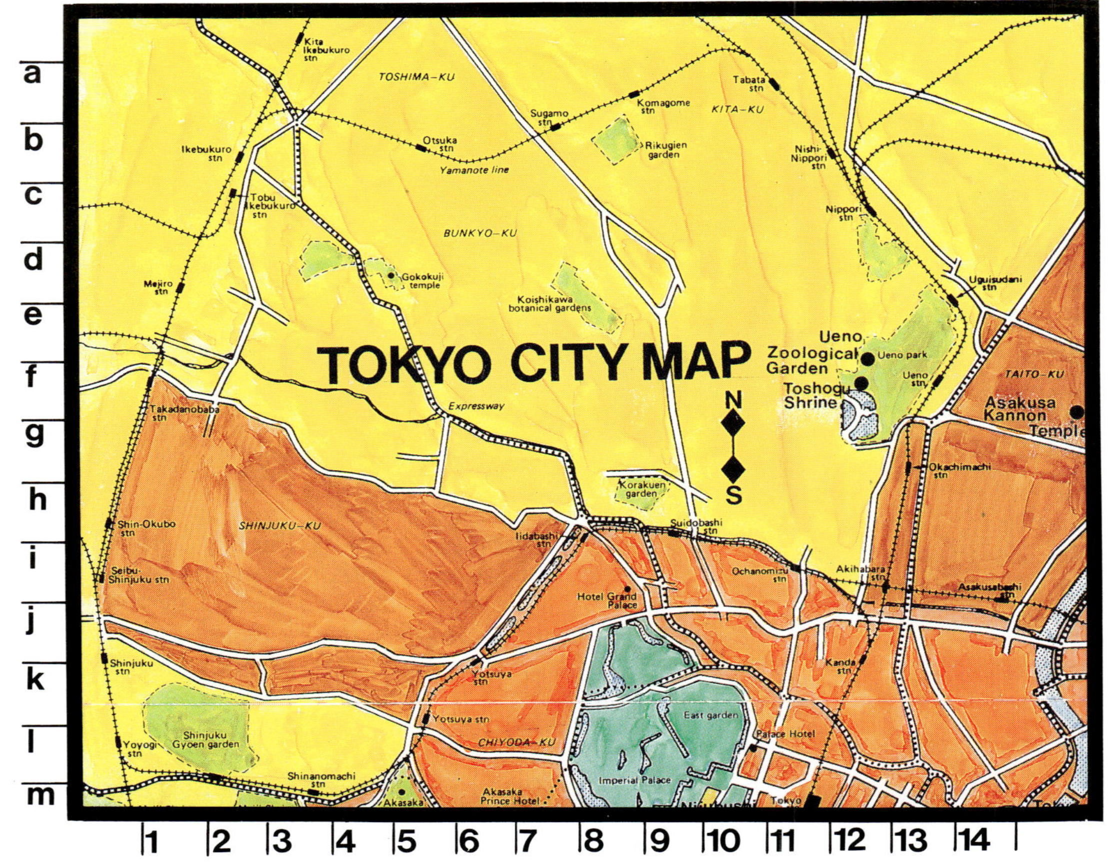

TOKYO CITY MAP
N
S
TOSHIMA-KU
KITA-KU
BUNKYO-KU
SHINJUKU-KU
CHIYODA-KU
TAITO-KU
Kita Ikebukuro stn
Ikebukuro stn
Tobu Ikebukuro stn
Otsuka stn
Yamanote line
Sugamo stn
Komagome stn
Rikugien garden
Tabata stn
Nishi-Nippori stn
Nippori stn
Uguisudani stn
Mejiro stn
Gokokuji temple
Koishikawa botanical gardens
Ueno Zoological Garden
Ueno park
Ueno stn
Toshogu Shrine
Asakusa Kannon Temple
Takadanobaba stn
Expressway
Okachimachi stn
Korakuen garden
Shin-Okubo stn
Suidobashi stn
Iidabashi stn
Seibu-Shinjuku stn
Ochanomizu stn
Akihabara stn
Asakusabashi stn
Hotel Grand Palace
Shinjuku stn
Yotsuya stn
Kanda stn
East garden
Palace Hotel
Yoyogi stn
Shinjuku Gyoen garden
Imperial Palace
Shinanomachi stn
Akasaka
Akasaka Prince Hotel
Tokyo
a
b
c
d
e
f
g
h
i
j
k
l
m
1 2 3 4 5 6 7 8 9 10 11 12 13 14

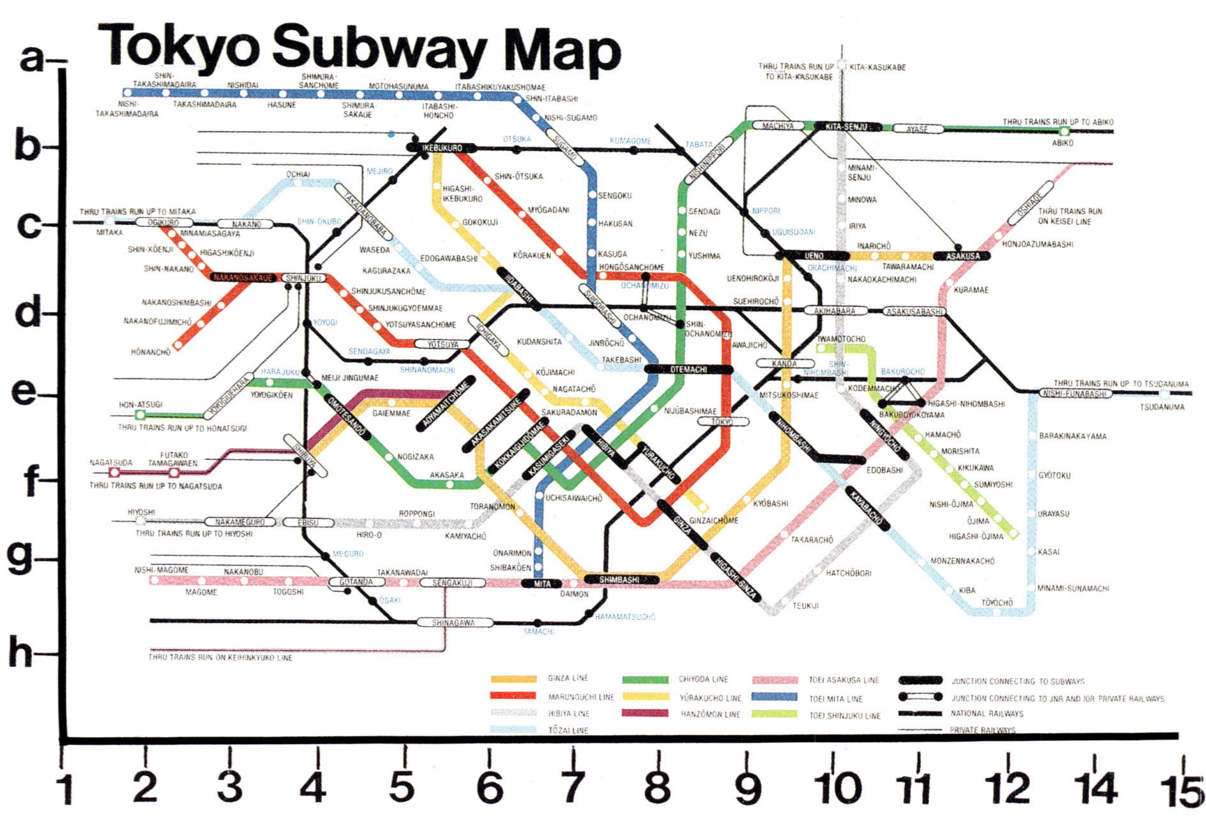

Tokyo Subway Map
THRU TRAINS RUN UP TO KITA-KASUKABE
KITA-KASUKABE
THRU TRAINS RUN UP TO ABIKO
ABIKO
THRU TRAINS RUN UP TO MITAKA
MITAKA
THRU TRAINS RUN ON KEISEI LINE
THRU TRAINS RUN UP TO TSUDANUMA
TSUDANUMA
THRU TRAINS RUN UP TO HONATSUGI
THRU TRAINS RUN UP TO NAGATSUDA
THRU TRAINS RUN UP TO HIYOSHI
THRU TRAINS RUN ON KEIHINKYUKO LINE
GINZA LINE
MARUNOUCHI LINE
HIBIYA LINE
TŌZAI LINE
CHIYODA LINE
YŪRAKUCHO LINE
HANZŌMON LINE
TOEI ASAKUSA LINE
TOEI MITA LINE
TOEI SHINJUKU LINE
JUNCTION CONNECTING TO SUBWAYS
JUNCTION CONNECTING TO JNR AND/OR PRIVATE RAILWAYS
NATIONAL RAILWAYS
PRIVATE RAILWAYS
a
b
c
d
e
f
g
h
1 2 3 4 5 6 7 8 9 10 11 12 14 15

"It sure is hot and humid," said Mom.

"At least being underground with the train windows open creates a bit of a breeze," replied Dad.

I was so hot I yelled out: "I'm sweating. I mean perspiring!"

Kenny laughed. "You'll get used to it! This is one of life's facts that we Japanese simply try to accept!"

"I don't think I'll ever get used to this heat," I protested. It was more like thirty-four degrees Celsius than the average twenty-eight degrees Celsius.

I had a funny thought. I knew people were looking at us and yet when I looked at them they were all looking at their feet or staring off into space. Kenny must have read my thoughts.

"My dad calls it 'seeing without looking'!" he said. "In earlier times, the Japanese built their homes with paper and bamboo to reduce the danger of injury during earthquakes and typhoons. Because of these thin walls, they were forced to learn how to create a private space within the mind. In modern Japan, people use this skill to cope with the large crowds and to respect each other's need for privacy."

"They almost create walls with their minds," Dad added.

Mom added that I would understand this better when we visited a Japanese garden and the Adachi's home.

"It must be like trying to watch T.V. while Dad is asleep and snoring on the couch!" I replied.

"Very funny," replied Dad with a wink to Kenny.

I had lots of questions but before I could ask any of them we had arrived at Ueno Station.

"Lorraine, you have to hurry or the train will continue on with you still on board!" Kenny warned.

We walked out of Ueno Station to begin our first real day of discovering Tokyo and *Nihon*.

We went into a popular shopping area. There was a sign in *Romaji* telling us we were in the Ueno Shopping Area. One section of the shopping area had modern western clothes for sale, another had open air fish and vegetable markets. Kenny explained that even though almost all homes have refrigerators most people still like to buy their fish and vegetables fresh each day. As we walked between the rows of stalls I thought of the farmers' market back home. The rows of stalls seemed to go on forever. There were many different things for sale. Kenny pointed out the vegetables, fish, cakes, and other things that were completely new and different to me. Each merchant was trying to convince customers to buy their goods. *ICHIBAN* (*ee•chee•bohn* - number one) was the cry!

One lady, dressed in a pretty summer *KIMONO* (*kee•mo•noh* - Japanese robe), offered me a *MOCHI* (*mo•chee* - Japanese pastry), which is a rice cake stuffed with bean curd. It looked like a small jelly roll with a pretty sesame seed design on top. I hesitantly thanked the lady and bit into my *mochi*. "*Ichiban, domo arigato*," I said. It really tasted good, so I bought some more to take with me.

The noise and the smells gave the area a carnival atmosphere. Some smells were very strong and I had to resist the idea of plugging my nose. "The fish market does smell strong at first but you'll get used to it," Kenny said.

I replied that there were some smells that were just too strong to get used to. Kenny reminded me that I was the one who was not bothered by barnyard smells back home.

Kenny and I stopped to chat with a fisherman who spoke *Eigo*. He introduced himself as Sumio Sato.

"My *otoosan* was a fisherman and so was his *otoosan*. My *otoosan* taught me how to mend nets and clean fish," said Mr. Sato. "He also taught me how to cook rice. I became the cook's helper on a fishing boat when I was only ten years old."

"Fishing must be one of the only areas that modern technology hasn't affected," I commented.

To my surprise, Mr. Sato replied, "No, you are quite wrong. Even the simple occupation of fishing has changed over the years. When I was a boy, for example, we used to set the nets close to the shore. We would check these at the end of each day. We would also go to the fishing areas far out in the ocean. Now, other fishing nations have made laws that limit where we may fish. There is also much book work involved. I much prefer the simple task of mending the nets."

I looked around the crowded market; it seemed to hold so much tradition. "But the way you sell the fish must still be the same," I said.

Mr. Sato smiled. "Even this has changed over the years," he said. "We used to sell all of our fish to buyers who would come to our village. Many of the local families would share in the catch. Today, we must pack our catch on ice and ship it to Tsukiji Market in Tokyo. At this market the fish are bought and sold for use throughout Japan. The prices change greatly from day to day. Millions of tons of fish are caught each year. Nowadays, there are even fish farms in the shallow waters."

I was puzzled. "Fish farms?" I asked. "What are those?"

"My friend Akiro is a fish farmer," replied Mr. Sato. "He raises shrimp, scallops, eels, and oysters. He must feed them every day and harvest them when they are ready. He keeps records of how much he feeds them and how much they weigh. He is not a fisherman; he is a farmer. As for me," he continued with a shrug, "if I wanted to be a farmer, I would rather grow rice."

Kenny entered the conversation. "There must be some ways in which modern inventions have helped you," he said.

"Yes," admitted Mr. Sato, "I like many of the new inventions, especially my fiberglass boat and gasoline engine. However, I still believe that technology is harmful to my trade." He sighed and told us: "The other day I went to check my shallow nets. They were covered in oil. I wish people in Tokyo would worry more about fixing their leaky ships that haul this black slime than making rules about my fishing. The oil is killing the fish. More and more I must travel farther out to sea to catch the fish. The Sea of Okhotsk and the Bering Sea are becoming the main fishing grounds for the Japanese fisherman."

There was a long pause, and then Kenny blurted out, "Did you ever hunt whales?"

I thought it was a dumb question, but Mr. Sato did not laugh. "No, I haven't," he answered, "but my uncle is a whaler. He has just left for a long trip to Australia."

I was shocked. "I thought whale hunting was illegal," I said.

Mr. Sato looked sad. "There are many people throughout the world who do not want us to eat the whales," he said. "Even though we use every part of the whale, we are told this is not right. Each month my uncle receives letters and newspaper articles that tell him his way of life is wrong. He tells me that he will always be a whaler because it is all he knows," Mr. Sato concluded.

I gave him one of my *mochi* and we said our good-byes. As we left the marketplace, I thought about how the modern ideas and technology have affected simpler ways of life. I made a note to myself to include this in my report.

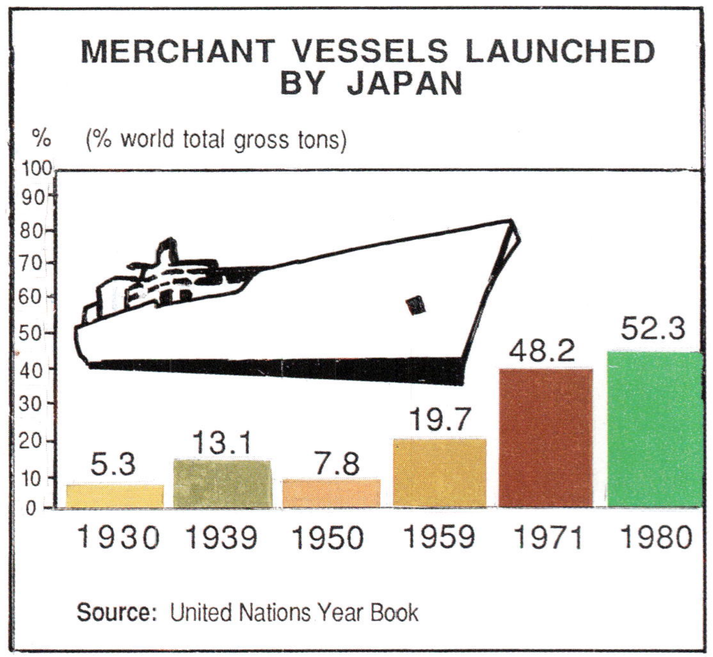

A Shinto Shrine in Nihon is easily recognized.

A Buddhist Temple in Japan.

We went to the ***Ueno Zoological Garden***. Many people were there in order to escape the heat and the rapid pace of the city. Kenny pointed out a shrine. He explained that a **Shinto Shrine** in *Nihon* is easily recognized by the double cross pieces of wood supported by two large wooden poles. **Buddhist Temple** entrances have large wooden doors and walls.

We paid ¥300 each for an entrance ticket to the Rinonji Temple. Even the ticket looked like a work of art. The *okane* is used to maintain and **restore** the building. We entered the wooden building at the end of a walkway. The area around the building was so calm and peaceful. The garden-like setting made it seem as if we were in the country and not in the city. Before we went into the main temple building we took off our shoes. This act symbolized two *Nihonjin* beliefs. One was related to cleanliness and the other to leaving the outside world outside.

Then we visited a Shinto shrine called the ***Toshogu Shrine***. The interior had many gold-plated walls and doors. Kenny pointed out the formal area for prayer. A man was standing before the altar and he clapped his hands together three times. This was to let those he was praying to know that he was there. The building itself was separated into two areas. There was a formal area for prayer and a large room with historical items.

As we walked through the park we saw a little boy trying to feed the pigeons. I remember saying that this is one place where no one seems to be in a hurry. Dad noticed that everyone seemed to be smiling – even in the heat!

We started back towards Ueno Station. Before we left the park Mom spotted an area set up for a Japanese tea ceremony. Kenny suggested that his mom would explain and show us the importance of the tea ceremony to the Japanese culture when we visited his home.

When we were close to Ueno Station Mom pointed out the movie theaters. Kenny said that they usually rent video movies instead of going to the theater because a movie usually costs ¥1500.

"At those prices I'd watch a video too!" I replied.

"Look!" yelled Kenny. "A video-game arcade! Let's go in and get out of the heat. You can feel the air conditioning working from here!"

"This building next to it has different games and lots of bright lights. What is it?" I asked.

"That's a **Pachinko** parlor," replied Kenny.

Dad noticed that the Pachinko parlors seemed to be full of adults only. "Lorraine, you and Kenny can play the video games while your mother and I check out these other games."

I asked Kenny what Pachinko was.

"It's kind of like an upright pinball game," he answered. "You pay about ¥100 for twenty silver balls, and then you try to get them to go into little slots and holes so that you can win more balls. Then you trade the balls that you've won for candy and other prizes. Some people trade their prizes for money at exchange places outside the Pachinko parlors," he explained.

A half hour passed and then Mom and Dad found us playing a video game. On the way out we told them about the boy in the leather jacket that asked us if we wanted to buy drugs.

Kenny told us that the pressure is not as great in *Nihon* as in North America for teenagers to use drugs. Most children and teenagers realize that drugs are dangerous to their health. And besides, the disgrace that one would bring to their family would be very great. "No one would act foolishly if it meant **losing face**!" Kenny exclaimed.

"How could you lose your face?" I asked in disbelief.

Dad laughed. "Kenny didn't really mean that you would lose your face. Only that the family **honor** or status would be affected by the behavior of any one of its members. Behaving in a socially acceptable manner is very important in *Nihon*."

It was almost 4:00 P.M. when we got back on the silver colored ***Hibiya Line*** subway train and returned to the hotel. After supper we took the subway to Ginza Station. At last I was going to see the famous and modern Ginza shopping area of Tokyo! We took an escalator to the main street and discovered that we were right in the heart of the Ginza District. I yelled: "Look at all the neon signs! It's like Las Vegas!"

We decided to walk up and down the main street. There was so much to see! The people were dressed in business suits, traditional summer *YUKATA* (*yuh•kah•tah* -Japanese dress), silk dresses (always with nylons), designer jeans, and school uniforms.

Kenny laughed. "You'll get a sore neck with all your turning from one side to the other. Now you can begin to see what I meant by the 'two roads to travel' in discovering *Nihon*."

Just then Mom said to Dad: "Look Ted – a *GEISHA*! " (*gee•shah* - Japanese lady artist/performer).

"The lady certainly is dressed in a traditional *kimono* and is walking slightly behind the man in the business suit," Dad replied, "but she may be his wife and not a *geisha*!"

"I think she's beautiful!" I said.

Kenny shocked us all by sighing, "Me too!" He blushed as soon as he realized what he had said.

"Mr. Adachi has promised to take us to an older part of Tokyo so that we can see a tea house and watch a performance by the *geisha*s!" Dad said. "Visitors rarely get to see the accomplished musicians, dancers, and trained entertainers perform the traditional dances and ceremonies. Often they simply see the commercial shows," he added.

"The real *geisha* is like a very well trained artist and one of the last remaining symbols of traditional Japanese society," Kenny said.

I made a note to ask Mrs. Adachi more about the *geisha* lady we had seen.

As we walked along I was looking at the highrises and suddenly saw the Golden Arches on a tall thin building. I said to Kenny: "You really do have McDonald's in Tokyo!"

"Sure," he replied. "Before I went to the United States I thought McDonald's was only in Japan."

Dad said to Mom in a laughing voice: "Remember Mrs. Adachi telling us that many of the children have grown up thinking that McDonald's and Wendy's hamburgers are Japanese food!"

There are several large department stores in the Ginza District. The mannequins in the window of the Matsuzakaya Department Store were blondes and brunettes wearing the latest in Western styles.

"Now I understand what you were saying on the plane about the models!" I said to Kenny.

"There seem to be a lot of businessmen in these small restaurants and beer halls. Have you noticed that there are only groups of men?" I heard Mom say to Dad.

Dad replied: "The men and women seem to go places in separate groups."

I knew what Mom was thinking. I couldn't wait to ask Mrs. Adachi about the role of women in *Nihon*.

We went from Ginza to our Kodenmacho Station in two minutes.

When we got to the street it seemed like every car on the road had a taxi light on top. Right out in front of our hotel a man was serving four other men bowls of *UDON* (*oo•dohn* - noodle) from a wooden wagon kitchen on wheels.

The hotel staff greeted us, bowed and handed us our room keys. When we got to our rooms we turned on the television. There was a little switch that allowed us to hear our program in *Eigo*.

I asked Kenny: "Why don't they have all programs available as bilingual broadcasts?"

"Probably the cost," he replied. "For most of these shows it really does not matter. I can tell you the important things. Besides, you'll learn more *Nihongo* this way!"

We watched a game show where kids got covered with tubs of flour if they guessed the wrong answer. Different things were thrown between two doors or screens and they had to guess what it was. The first person to hit the buzzer got to guess first. The person with the most correct guesses won. The person who guessed wrong got covered in flour – lots of flour! They threw *hashi*, fans, stuffed animals, fish, boxes, and even had a baby walk between the doors.

I laughed and said to Kenny: "You were right! I can understand what's going on without knowing a word!"

"Laughter is the same the world over and so is bedtime," Mom added. "Finish your *ocha* and then it's off to bed. Say good-night, you two!"

We both yelled: "*Oyasumi nasai.*"

Dad's reply from his bed was "ZZZZZzzzz...!"

"I hope the sound of the sleeping bear doesn't keep you awake!" I whispered to Kenny.

"I'm used to it!" he replied. "It was nice in Beaver Creek to have thick walls. But at home in Tokyo, and in our old house in Sapporo, my Dad's snoring could be heard throughout the house. In fact, I'm surprised the neighbors didn't complain."

I drifted off to sleep with a vision of the lights of Ginza in my dream and then the image of the silent waves in the sea of sand in the rock garden of the Toshogu Shrine.

Chapter 4

FROM EDO TO TOKYO

JAPANESE VOCABULARY

WORDS

bunraku	bun•ra•kuh	puppet
bushido	boo•she•doh	Japanese code of honor
daimyo	day•myoh	Japanese noble
Edo	ee•doh	Old Japan
hibachi	hee•bah•chee	Japanese barbecue
ojiisan	oh•jee•sahn	grandfather
Kabuki	kah•boo•kee	traditional theatrical performance
Kami	kah•mee	gods
koto	koh•to	horizontal harp
koden	koe•den	gift of money
Noh	noh	Japanese classical drama
Ojiisan	oh•jee•sahn	grandfather
sake	sah•kee	rice wine
shakuhachi	shaw•coo•ha•chee	black and gold lacquered bamboo flute
shamisen	sha•mi•zen	Japanese guitar or lute
Samurai	sahm•oorh•iy	Japanese warrior
Shinto	shin•toh	Japanese religion
Shogun	show•gohn	chief military ruler of all Japan

PHRASES and SENTENCES:

San-san kudo	Sahn•sahn ku•doh	Part of a Japanese marriage salutation

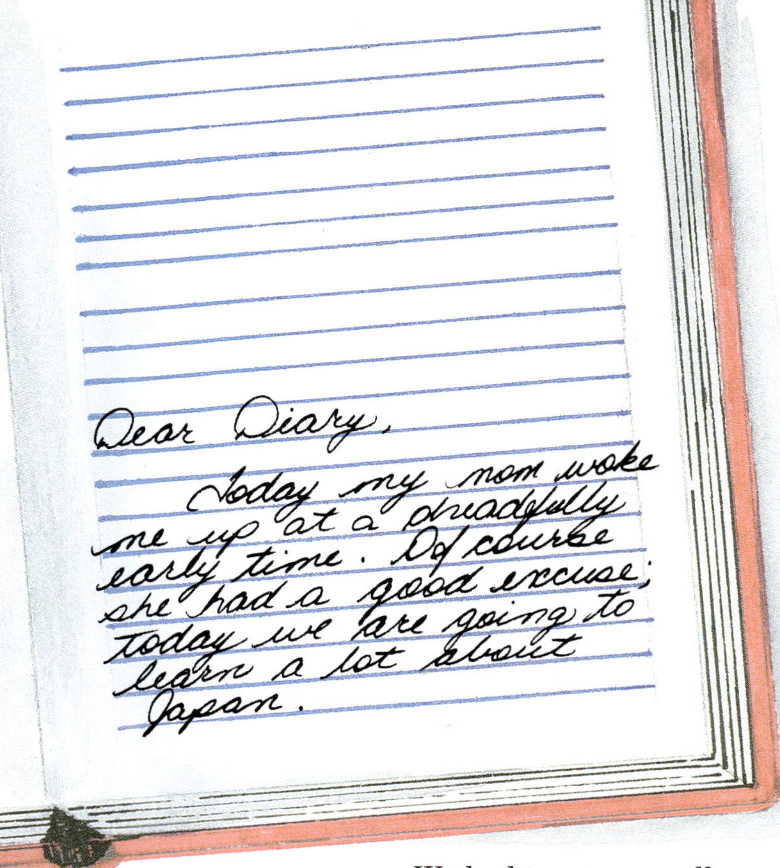

We had to get up really early to avoid the rush hour crowds at the subway station. Some stations are so busy that they have to use "people pushers." These are the men with white gloves who actually push passengers onto the trains so that the doors can close.

Kenny knocked, then popped his head in through the door and sang out a cheerful: "*Ohayo gozaimasu*."

We all replied: "*Konnichi wa*!"

"Well, is everybody ready to discover *EDO*?"(*ee•doh* - old Japan) Dad said.

"What's *Edo*?" I asked.

Dad winked at Kenny and replied: "The old road to *Nihon*! *Edo* was the capital of feudal *Nihon*."

I was confused. "What do you mean by 'feudal'?" I asked.

"In old *Nihon* the Imperial Family and the nobles owned all of the land in *Nihon*," Kenny explained.

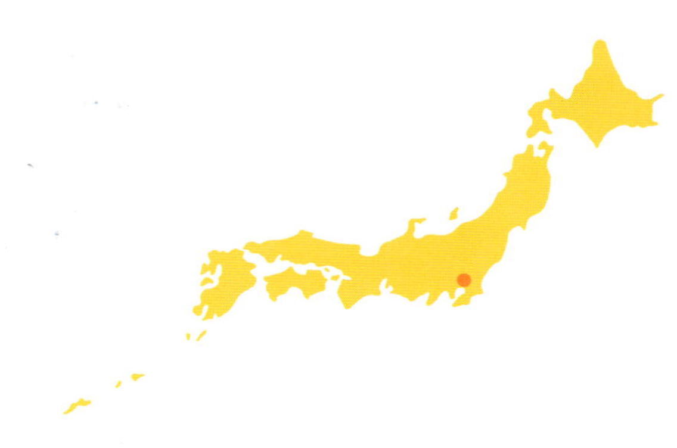

FEUDALISM IN JAPAN

Shogunate or military government began with the warrior Minamoto-no-Yoritomo, the leader of a powerful *samurai* clan. He took over the country in 1185 and seven years later was given the title of *Seii-Taishogun*, or Barbarian-quelling General. For the next five hundred years, it was the Shogun, not the Emperor, who ruled Japan. The Emperor retained his title and castle, but had no real authority.

As time went on, military unrest became common. *Samurai* leaders took over the land of the nobles and became *DAIMYO* (*day•myoh* - Japanese lord), or feudal lords.

The nobles were allowed to live peacefully, and were able to develop their skills in the noble disciplines of **art, writing, music, and meditation**.

When a *daimyo* and his *samurai* defeated all the other *daimyo* in battle, he was given the title of *shogun* and was the military ruler of all Japan.

"Were nobles in *Nihon* like nobles in early England?" I asked.

"Yes, sort of," said Dad.

"Did they live in castles?" I wondered.

"Yes, they did," Kenny replied. "The area around each castle was built to make it difficult to get to by direct path. In this way hostile armies would get lost and be easy prey for the *SAMURAI.*" (*sahm•oorh•iy* - Japanese warrior).

Dad interrupted: "So that's why Tokyo is such a confusing city to drive around in. There isn't a straight road in the whole city!"

Kenny disagreed: "The new expressways try to make driving easier and more efficient but *Edo* really did have streets like a maze. You have to remember that it was not until after World War II that *Nihon* really started to build cars and fill its roads with them."

"Wait a minute!" I said, "Were the *samurai* like the knights of medieval Europe? What happened to the Imperial family?"

"Lorraine," Kenny said, "I'll sit down with you and draw a chart or picture to sort this out. We can also make a time line for the history of *Nihon*."

After hearing all this I couldn't wait for our day to begin. Modern-day Tokyo, from what I had seen, was much like any other big city except almost everyone here was Japanese and spoke *Nihongo*. Now we were going to travel the old way and discover its traditions.

We took the subway to the Holiday Inn. Our tour guide, a lady named Yoko, met us in the lobby. She indicated that we would travel by taxi to the Imperial Palace. Yoko spoke *Eigo* very well. She had been to the United States many times to visit her Aunt who lives in Idaho. I told her that we would be able to discover modern Tokyo on our other days, and that today we wanted to see and hear the traditions of *Edo*.

"Well then," Yoko said, "let's get out and begin!"

I looked up and saw that we were parked beside a large river and a huge wall. In my excitement I forgot about the automatically closing door on the taxi and slammed it shut. The driver was not amused.

"The palace is where *Edo* Castle used to be," Yoko said. "You must remember that Tokyo has been destroyed many times over by earthquakes and floods. *Nihon* is a land that was built by volcanoes and is often reduced to rubble by the earthquakes. In 1923 there was a huge earthquake. Of course, the city was reduced to rubble once again in 1945 by the air raid bombings and fires."

"We grew up with Japanese-Americans who suffered through the internment and know the tragedies of the war," Mom said. "We also know of Pearl Harbor and the devastation of the bombings there. It is amazing that two countries acted in ways that caused such loss of life in these

THE SAMURAI

Samurai were warriors who lived by a very complex set of rules called *BUSHIDO* (*boo•she•doh* - Japanese code of honor).Their beliefs in honor, bravery, sacrifice, health and discipline were passed on from generation to generation. The *samurai* were born *samurai*, and could be men or women. *Samurai* women were trained to use weapons, although they did not participate in battles. They were also responsible for the household. These *samura*i women often made sure that the peasants grew the crops in a manner to ensure the well-being of all.

As time went on the *samurai* became more skilled in the disciplines of martial arts, meditation, and the teachings of Buddhism.

JAPAN TIME LINE

JOMON PERIOD
3000 B.C. Hunting & gathering

YAMATO PERIOD
300 A.D. Introduction of Buddhism

NIRA PERIOD
710 Est. of Capital of Heijo (present Nara)
752 Dedication of Todai-ji Great Buddha (in Nara)

KAMAKURA PERIOD
1192 Est. of Kamakura Shogunate

MUROMACHI PERIOD
1543 Coming of Portuguese
1549 Est. of Christian Mission

EDO PERIOD
1603 Est. of Tokugawa Shogunate by Tokugawa Ieyasu

古代　飛鳥　奈良　平安　鎌倉　室町　安土桃山　江戸

ca. 3000 B.C. Civilization emerges, centered along Indus, Nile & Yellow rivers
27 B.C. Est. of Roman Empire
622 A.D. Islamic era begins
1215 Signing of Magna Carta in England
1275 Marco Polo reaches China
ca. 1450 Invention of printing press by Gutenburg
1492 Columbus reaches America
1775 War of Independance in the United States
1789 French Revolution

WORLD TIME LINE

places of great beauty. Fortunately, the city seems complete. How did the old survive along with the new? We have seen both."

"The modern parts have been built since the war. The old has been rebuilt many times over," Yoko replied. "One of the unique traditions of the Japanese is to accept 'bad luck' and disasters, both natural and man-made, and to simply rebuild."

"We have rebuilt and restored the house of my *OJIISAN* (*oh•jee•sahn* - grandfather) six times," Kenny added. "Each time he insisted that we rebuild it in the same place. The last time we also built a shrine. His ashes are at rest there now."

Yoko continued with her explanation: "As a little girl I was told by my *obaasan* and *okaasan* that I should not waste time wondering why things happened but should plan on what to do next."

Japanese accept disasters and simply rebuild.

NATURAL DISASTERS

There are approximately 170 volcanoes in Japan, some 25 of which have erupted since 1850 or remain active. Earthquakes add to the unstable nature of the land. Japan has more earthquakes than any other country in the world. Modern instruments can detect up to 7,500 earthquakes a year. Forty to fifty of these are of enough force to be perceptible to humans. In some parts of Japan, major destructive earthquakes occur once every two years.

EDO AND THE TOKUGAWA SHOGUNATE

In 1603 a man named Ieyasu Tokugawa brought his army to the small fishing village of Edo and established a military government thus beginning the Edo period.

SHOGUN (*show•gohn* - chief military ruler of all Japan) Tokugawa closed Japan to outside influences for over 240 years. During this time there was peace in Japan, and the country did not borrow or adapt new ideas from other countries again until after 1853. In 1868, at the start of the Meiji Era, Imperial rule was restored. Edo was then renamed Tokyo and became the eastern capital of *Nihon*. Kyoto became the western capital.

Ieyasu Tokugawa was a Japanese Shogun.

"Hey, that is really neat," said Kenny. "My *ojiisan* used to tell me not to say 'if only' but rather 'now I will'."

I remember thinking that this was truly the spirit of *Edo*.

"The present palace was rebuilt in 1968," Yoko said. "It had been restored in 1888 as part of the **Meiji Era** or **Restoration**. The path around the palace is now a popular jogging trail.

MODERN PERIOD
1853 Arrival of Commodore Perry
1868 Restoration of Imperial Rule
1904 Russo-Japanese War
1923 Tokyo Earthquake
1941 Outbreak of Pacific War
1945 Atomic bombings of Hiroshima & Nagasaki
1947 Pop. of Japan 78 million
1952 End of Allied Occupation
1956 Admission of Japan to United Nations
1972 Sapporo Olympic Games
1986 Tokyo Economic Summit
1986 Pop. of Japan 120.75 Million

明 治 大 正 昭 和 戦 後

1879 Invention of electric light by Edison
1914-18 First World War
1939-45 Second World War
1940 Pop. of U.S. 132 million
1950-53 Korean War
1975 End of Vietnam War
1980 Pop. of U.S. 226 Million

"Normally the public is only allowed over the main ***Nijubushi Bridge*** and into the private grounds on two days each year. These two are New Year's Day and April 29 – the Emperor's birthday. However, today we are very lucky. There are three families of Japanese farmers who have travelled to Tokyo on their holiday. One of them is my uncle. They are spending two days of their holiday taking care of the Palace's East Garden. They do this as a voluntary gift of respect for the Emperor and his family. They consider it an honor to be able to serve the Imperial family."

"Why would they volunteer to garden during their holiday? Isn't there some other way to show respect?" I had to ask.

Yoko laughed. "Of course, there are many ways to show respect! I'll try to explain why gardening is important. Do you know what a *samurai* is?"

"*Hai*!" I proudly answered.

"Well then," Yoko continued, "you know that *samurai* are usually born into a family of *samurai*. However my great-grandfather was a farmer who became a *samurai* because an Emperor rewarded him with land and peasants."

"What was he rewarded for?" Dad asked Yoko.

Yoko responded by saying that her great-grandfather had taken up arms to protect a member of the Imperial family when a *daimyo* tried to take some of its family members as hostages.

"Then you are a *samurai* too!" I said.

Yoko replied: "There are no longer *samurai* in *Nihon* but I still try to live by the customs, beliefs and teachings of my ancestors. My uncle is also *samurai* but chose to return to farming."

"Now we must hurry if we are to be present when the Emperor meets the 'Imperial gardeners'."

Mom was amazed. "You mean the Emperor is going to meet with them and us?"

"It is a simple way to say thank you and reward their labor and loyalty," Yoko said with a smile.

The gardens were beautiful. Yoko explained that what I thought was a river was a moat. It was like a canal that went in a circle around the castle. The castle walls were made of huge rocks.

As we walked along the paths I kept thinking how peaceful and pretty everything was. Every bush and tree seemed perfectly formed. Every blade of grass appeared to be in exactly the right place. We came upon ten or twelve *Nihonjin* dressed in white. They all had white scarves over their heads and were wearing gloves. They were filling wicker baskets with dead leaves and branches.

Yoko introduced us to her uncle, Mr. Fusa Endo. He was the tallest and thinnest Japanese man I had seen in *Nihon*. He also had the biggest and nicest smile of anyone I had ever met.

Just as we were introduced to everyone and beginning to share stories, two very big men in grey military uniforms appeared. A third man in

JAPAN'S EMPEROR

The late Emperor Hirohito, shown here with his granddaughter, was the world's longest reigning monarch. Born in 1901, he became Emperor in 1926 and reigned until his death in 1989. Upon his death, his son Akihito became the 125th Emperor of Japan. Akihito was officially enthroned on November 22, 1990.

The Emperor is the symbol of the State and of the unity of the people; he has no powers related to government. His role is much the same as that of the Queen of England.

The reigning Emperor and Empress traditionally attend numerous events such as tree-planting ceremonies held every spring and the National Sports Festival held in autumn. They also attend exhibitions and concerts to express their support of cultural, social, and educational endeavors.

The Imperial Palace in Tokyo.

a blue uniform approached Mr. Endo. He asked everyone to move from the garden area to the paved pathway. An older man with a moustache and wearing a dark blue business suit approached us.

Formal bows were exchanged and a lot of words we could not understand. I just remember the kind face of the Emperor and his warm words, in *Eigo*, of welcome.

We went for lunch at Chinzanso Garden Restaurant. Yoko said that this was a popular place for weddings. "I will be twenty-nine in another year and I am hoping that my fiancé and I will be married here. Most of my friends are already married," she told us.

Our lunch was prepared on a modern *HIBACHI* (*hee•bah•chee* - Japanese barbecue). In the days of *Edo* the iron *hibachi* bowl was heated by coals. The cooking grill being used today was heated by gas.

The meal was delicious. I continued to improve at using the *hashi*.

"There are over 350 million pairs of *hashi* used in *Nihon* every month! That's one reason why Nihon must import so much lumber and wood. Right now some of our companies are trying to set up factories that will make *hashi* in North America, to be used in *Nihon*," said Yoko.

As we strolled through the garden area and stopped in front of the waterfall, Yoko began to tell us about weddings in *Nihon*. "Couples in *Nihon* marry for love. In the days of *Edo*, couples may have married because of an arrangement. Today, many people still believe, wrongly, that marriages are arranged when children are very young.
Some couples do meet through formal introductions but each has a choice to continue or end the relationship. Many people in *Nihon* may go through ten to fourteen formal introductions before meeting someone they want to date further, and then marry. The success rate for couples that marry as the result of an arranged formal introduction is about

the same as for those who meet by chance."

"All of this is interesting," I said, "but what I want to know about is the wedding ceremony!"

"Japanese couples can be married in either a Buddhist or a *SHINTO* (*shin•toh* - Japanese religion) ceremony," she replied. "Since Buddhism is mainly concerned with one's well-being after death and *Shinto* with the present life, most couples are married *Shinto* and buried Buddhist.

"Most Japanese women want to be married before they are twenty-eight years old. It is also usual for a man to be older than his wife.

"The wedding ceremony is a time for the traditions of *Edo*. The bride rents or has a very elegant *kimono* made. Often it will be made of red, white, silver, and gold silk patterns. Instead of a veil the bride wears a white headband. The groom will wear a black or dark-colored *kimono*. Here in Chinzanso there are several weddings going on at the same time in different rooms. Sunday is a popular day for weddings. It is typical for weddings to be videotaped. At Japanese weddings it is a tradition to take a large group photo. Every relative on both sides of the family is included."

"When my uncle was married we all went in the wedding room, a great big hall, and sat along the walls. We were all looking into the center of the room," said Kenny.

"The bride and groom sit beside each other and a shrine maiden serves the bride the wine made from rice called *SAKE* (*sah•kee* - rice wine). After she takes three sips the server offers the cup to the groom who also takes three sips. Then the groom takes three sips from a second cup and then the bride drinks three sips from the second cup," Yoko added.

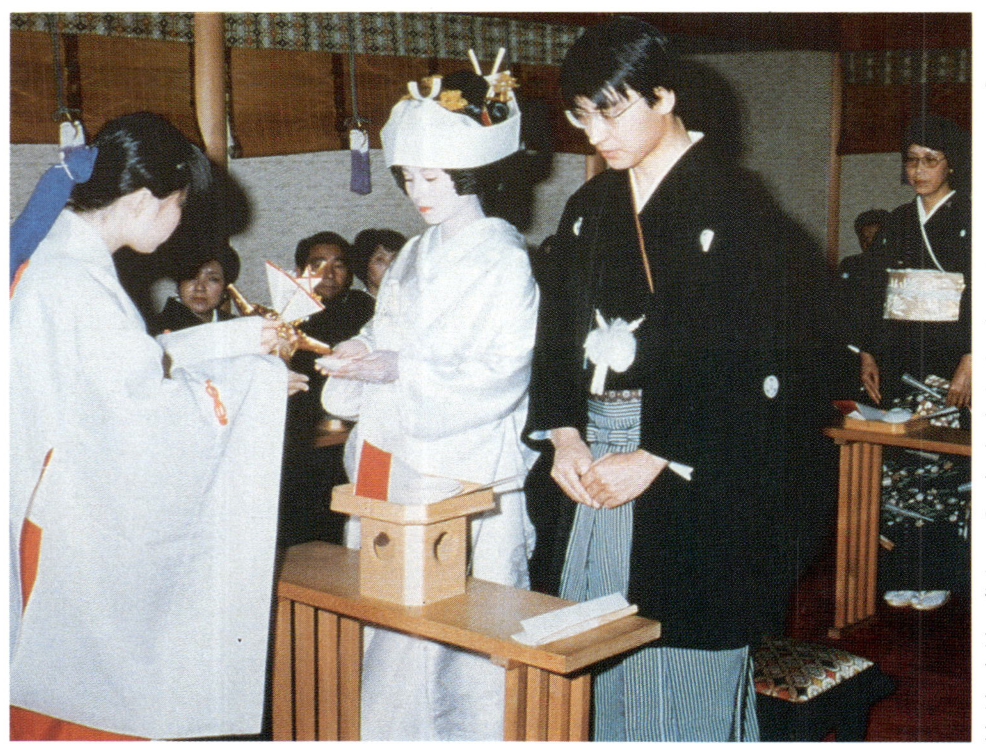

A Japanese wedding.

"And then what? Are they married?" I asked.

"No, the ceremony is called *SAN-SAN KUDO* (*san•san ku•doh* - marriage salutation)," replied Yoko. "It means three cups, three rounds, and nine sips each."

"So there must be one more cup and three more sips each!" I concluded with pride.

"That is right! After each has taken nine sips from the three cups they are married," Yoko continued. "After the ceremony the bride will often change into a western white wedding gown and the groom into a light-colored suit or tuxedo.

"The bride and groom and their parents will then pay for a huge banquet for all of the guests. This is a very expensive party. A wedding is considered to be a big reason for spending a lot of money! Guests give gifts and most also give money. The bridal couple thanks the guests by giving them small gifts in return," said Yoko.

"This is one more example of the gift-giving that Mr. Adachi told me about," I said to Mom.

"When my *ojiisan* died," Kenny said to Dad, "the people who came to the funeral gave *KODEN* (*koe•den* - a gift of money in a special envelope) to help with the expenses of the funeral. My father showed me the family book where we record how much is given by each family. Whenever someone in that family dies we take *koden* with us to the funeral."

I interrupted: "Let's talk about funerals later when we go to a temple. Right now I want Yoko to tell us more about the party and the honeymoon!"

"In modern *Nihon* many couples holiday in Hawaii or in your Rocky Mountains. Even today, however, some couples still can't afford their own home and many live with the husband's parents.

"I almost forgot to tell you that some couples also get married in a Christian church. When they are of that faith the ceremony is exactly the same as in the United States, even the exchanging of rings, except the priest speaks *Nihongo*!" added Yoko.

"It's time we continued on our way. Let's go to ***Asakusa*** next!" Dad said.

"The Asakusa Kannon Temple is one of the oldest Buddhist temples in *Nihon*. It was started in the seventh century," Yoko said.

"The ***Nakamise*** Shopping Arcade near the temple is very modern and yet full of old history," Kenny added.

I asked: "Is that the two roads of *Nihon*?"

"*Hai*!" replied Kenny.

As the taxi stopped in front of a busy shopping area Yoko continued: "In the days of *Edo* the merchants and farmers were allowed to set up stalls to sell items to visitors who were going to the temple. The descendants of these vendors now sell items to temple visitors in modern Tokyo."

As we walked towards the temple Kenny said: "There's a pilgrim!"

I immediately thought of Thanksgiving.

"The pilgrims often travel to worship at important shrines and temples. They are very religious men," Yoko explained. The man we saw was dressed in a black *kimono*, without a belt,

Japanese sipping ceremony.

wore a straw hat and looked like a statue.

The arcade was alive with people. "It really is very crowded," Mom said. "Let's make sure we stay together." Yoko suggested that we go directly to the temple and shop later.

"Look at all the people praying and worshiping!" I exclaimed.

Mom pointed out the Japanese ladies lighting incense candles.

"The smoke is supposed to heal your aches and pains," Kenny said.

Some people were involved in a ceremony in the temple, others were throwing offerings of *koka* into a chest and still others were ringing a bell.

We emerged from the shopping area with our hands full. Mom had bought toys, two *kimono*s and many other souvenirs. We found Kenny at a booth outside of the temple gate. An older man was showing Kenny how to play a *SHAKUHACHI* (*shaw•coo•ha•chee* - a black and gold lacquered bamboo flute). He was telling Kenny in *Nihongo* to stand tall, wet his lips and breathe out slowly. Yoko said that the music was from the island of Okinawa.

RELIGIONS

A Shinto shrine.

A Buddhist Temple.

Shinto is the only religion native to Japan. Its KAMI (*kah•mee* - gods) are looked to for direction in the present life. Respect for nature is an important aspect. Although Shinto emphasizes life on Earth, the dead are honored with offerings of fruit and flowers.

The Buddhist faith was borrowed from the Chinese. Buddhism advocates meditation and self-discipline to prepare for life after death.

Many Japanese have adopted Christianity. Some follow the teachings of all three religions combined.

Dad bought a *shakuhachi* for Kenny. He was able to play several notes with help from the kind man. The man took great care to place the flute in a cloth case and then wrap it in brightly colored paper. Like all of Mom's things, this purchase looked like a Christmas present. We were still discovering the ways of *Edo*.

Yoko announced: "We had better go to the *Kokuritsu Gekijo* (National Theater) and then on to the *KABUKI* (*Kah•boo•kee* - theatrical performance). The *Kabuki* has radio earphones so that you can follow in *Eigo*."

Mom said to Dad: "This is just like stories told in Shakespeare's plays. I am really enjoying it." The play was about a *daimyo* who had been betrayed by a *samurai* warrior. In the end the *daimyo* gave his life to save a princess.

As we were leaving our balcony seats Kenny said: "Some plays last as long as five hours. That's why you can buy food and drinks in the lobby."

I really liked the costumes and the set. When they made an island in the ocean, the cloth was made to move as if it were alive.

"It felt as if we were in the middle of all of the action!" Mom added.

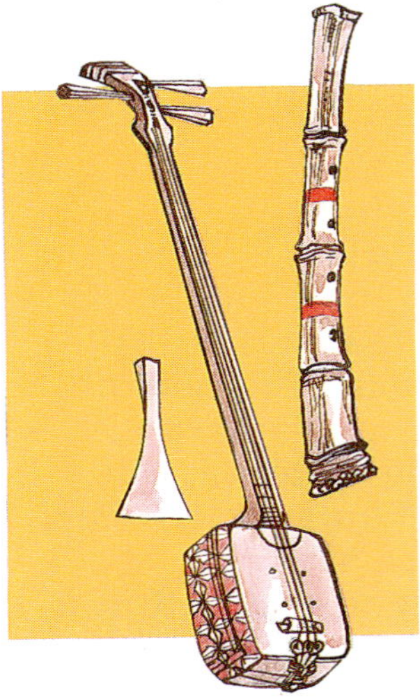

Japanese musical instruments.

"*Kabuki* is the most popular theater performance," Yoko said. "There is also *NOH* (*noh* - Japanese classical drama), where actors wear masks and chant rather than speak. When you go to Osaka you will also want to see a *BUNRAKU* (*bun•ra•kuh* - puppet) theater."

As we travelled towards Ginza I could still hear the music of the *SHAMISEN* (*sha•mi•zen* - a type of guitar) and the *KOTO* (*koh•to* - a kind of horizontal harp).

"Well that's enough of *Edo* for today," Dad said. "Tomorrow morning we will go up the ***Tokyo Tower*** and then visit the ***Meiji Shrine***. Mr. Adachi is meeting us for lunch and then taking us on a tour of some of *Nihon's* industries."

"Tomorrow evening we will go to the Adachis' home and then on to visit the *geishas* in an old tea house," added Mom.

I asked Yoko what she thought of Ginza. She replied: "Many of the things belonging to modern Tokyo are very interesting. In Ginza, I like the nightclubs, discos, the shopping, western clothes, modern music. On Sundays I enjoy strolling through the ***Harajuku*** district of Tokyo."

"Where is Harajuku?" I asked.

"It's near the Meiji Shrine in Ginza, which you will be seeing tomorrow. On Sundays, teenagers and young adults from all over Tokyo travel to Harajuku. We dress up in clothes like those of the Fifties in America!" she explained.

"That's why I was dressed up looking like Elvis Presley when I first met you in Beaver Creek," added Kenny.

"Harajuku is one place where the young people of *Nihon* are not controlled by the ways of *Edo*. The Japanese really are a fun-loving and happy people. Often they just wear a serious mask for outsiders. When you meet with Japanese people at play then you will really see the traditions of *Edo*. You see, *Edo* was truly built to bring sunshine into the lives of the hardworking people," said Yoko.

Kenny spotted a Shakey's Pizza Parlor. "If you really want to see smiling Japanese people, follow me!"

Before anyone could say anything Kenny was gone. We followed him down two flights of stairs and found ourselves in a pizza parlor. There were the usual wooden tables and chairs. There was disco and rock and roll music, lots of talking and laughter. A girl welcomed us and showed us to a table. We ordered pizzas and soft drinks by pointing to pictures in the self-serve menu. Our order number was called out, along with several others in *Nihongo*. Fortunately, Yoko heard our number being called. Everyone was smiling and laughing. I had never seen Japanese couples, families and groups having such a good time. It was great!

As we came back out onto the streets of Ginza the neon lights were like *Nihon*'s fireflies. The women walking on the streets were dressed in high fashion dresses now! The men were in dark colored business suits. Teenagers had taken off their school uniforms and were wearing T-shirts with bright slogans printed on them in *Eigo*.

Sunday afternoon in Harajuku Park.

Later, we went to bed and I thought of some of the things Yoko had told us on the way home. She had told us that Tokyo has a population of twelve million people. The immediate surrounding area has about 35 million people living and working in it. Housing is very expensive because the land is so scarce. Cars are maintained in near perfect condition because of special yearly inspections and special taxes. The school year in *Nihon* begins in April and goes until March. That is why we saw children playing volleyball and soccer on the school playgrounds. Boys often run five to ten kilometers around the Imperial Palace each day.

Edo was truly a place where the traditions of *Nihon* were valued and nurtured. *Nihon* is a country that has borrowed the best from other countries and cultures.

"*Oyasumi nasai!*"

Chapter 5

ON TOP OF THE WORLD

JAPANESE VOCABULARY

WORDS

Asagao	Ah•sah•gah•oh	Morning Glory Fair
butsudan	boot•sue•dahn	family altar
bonsai	bon•sai	dwarf tree
buyo	boo•yoe	dance
Chado	chah•doh	tea ceremony
chanoma	cha•noh•mah	main room of a house
futon	foo•tohn	sleeping mattress
genken	gen•kehn	porch
geta	gay•tah	outside shoes
Hozuki-ichi	Hoh•zoo•kee•ee•chee	Grand Cherry Fair
ikebana	ee•kay•bah•na	art of flower arrangement
ken	koen	regions
kotasu	koe•tah•soo	low table
maiko	mah•ee•koh	apprentice geisha
meishi	may•ee•she	business card
ofuro	oh•fuu•roh	tub
oiran	oh•ee•ran	elite
san	sahn	sir or madam (a suffix of respect)
tabi	tab•ee	socks
taiko	tie•koh	drum
tatami	tah•tah•mee	mat made of rice straw
torii	toe•reeh	gateway
zori	zoe•ree	house slippers

PHRASES and SENTENCES:

Konban wa	kohn•bahn wa	Good evening
Oagari kudasai	oh•ah•gah•ree coo•dah•sigh	Please step up
Ogenki desu ka?	oh•gen•kee day•su ka	How are you?

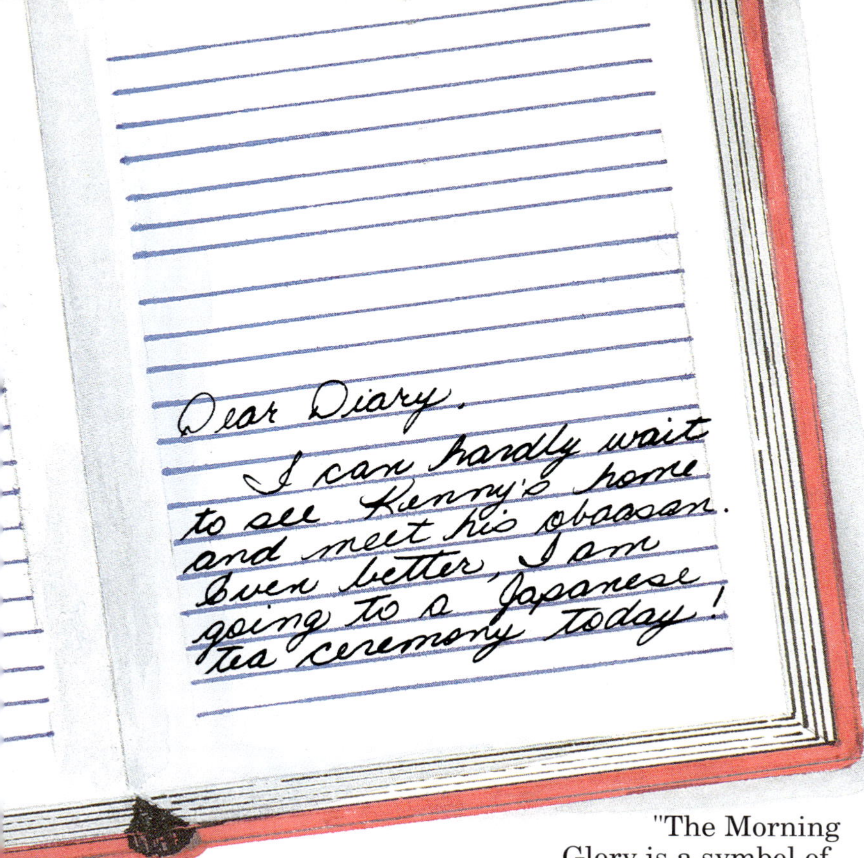

Kenny asked me if I remembered that the Emperor Meiji did much to modernize *Nihon*. Baseball and dancing came to *Nihon*, along with many other western traditions, during the Meiji era.

I was too busy looking at everything to respond.

"The Morning Glory is a symbol of summer," Kenny explained. "From July 6 to 8, a fair called *ASAGAO* (*ah•sah•gah•oh*- Morning Glory) is celebrated. On July 9 and 10 another fair called *HOZUKI-ICHI* (*hoh•zoo•kee-ee•chee* - Grand Cherry) will be set up at Asakusa Kannon Temple."

"That must be why the men were setting up those special stalls," Dad said.

From the top of the Tokyo Tower it seemed as if we could see all of *Nihon*. We could see temples, skyscrapers, shrines and expressways. Kenny told us that almost every city has a tower. They are modelled on the Eiffel Tower in Paris, France. On a clear day you can see ***Mt. Fuji*** from here, but we would see it better when we went to Kyoto and Osaka.

Dad pointed out the Meiji Shrine. It was a large green wooded area. "I read that the shrine is dedicated to the Emperor Meiji and his Empress Shoken. When we go there we will pass beneath a huge *TORII* (*toe•reeh* - gateway) made of 1,700-year-old cypress trees," he said.

The Tokyo Tower.

Mount Fuji.

There were golf practice ranges surrounded by very high nets and swimming pools with bleachers around them. People were moving everywhere.

After visiting the Meiji Shrine we met Mr. Adachi. He smiled and said: "*Konnichi wa,* Lorraine." And I replied: "*Ohayo gozaimasu!*"

Mr. Adachi asked Kenny if he was behaving himself. "I've been very good and am having a lot of fun!" Kenny replied.

Mr. Adachi said that first we would go to an automobile assembly plant. Then we would pick up Mrs. Adachi at her work. We would have supper at a very special restaurant and then visit a real Japanese tea house in the Asakusa area.

On the way to our first stop Mr. Adachi said: "*Nihon* has the pleasant problem of having a very rich economy. Right now we **export** more than we **import**. You will read in the papers that many countries want us to buy more products from them so that there will be a balance. That was one of my jobs in Beaver Creek. One of my Japanese clients wants to buy more log homes and build them in Hokkaido."

"Is the car industry still a major reason for *Nihon's* success?" Dad asked Mr. Adachi.

"Companies like Toyota, Honda, Suzuki, and Nissan did very well after the war," Mr. Adachi answered. "They remain leaders among *Nihon's* main **manufacturing** companies. These car companies borrowed a lot of money to get started. Yet, many of Japan's leading bankers did not think they could compete with North American companies like Ford and General Motors.

"Now," Mr. Adachi continued, "Toyota makes more money by investing its profits in land and financing other businesses than it does selling cars. Many of the big Japanese companies are buying the **stocks** of North American companies."

"I read where the Tokyo Stock Exchange is now equivalent to the New York and London Exchanges," Dad said. "That sure is a long way from the days of *Edo*!"

"In Japan we have almost every industry found throughout the world. Foreign visitors brought their ideas to our country. Today we use computers, videos, televisions, satellites and visits to other countries to discover new ideas and ways of doing things," continued Mr. Adachi.

After Emporer Meiji and his Empress died, this shrine was built.

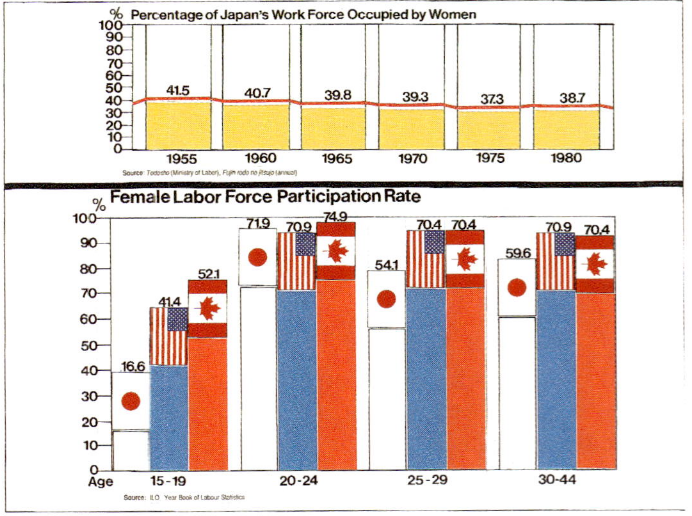

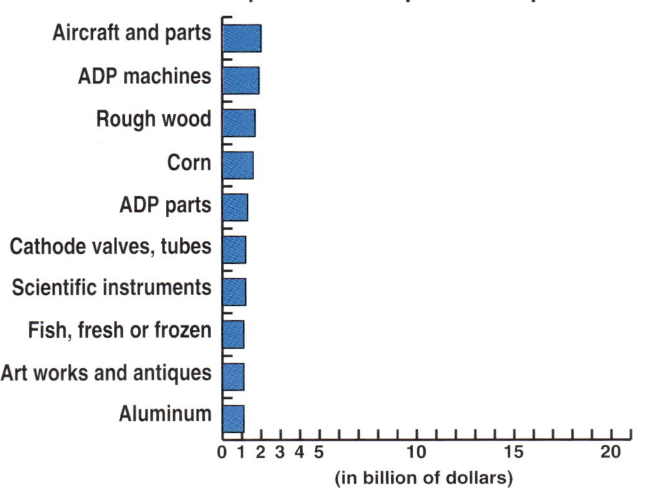

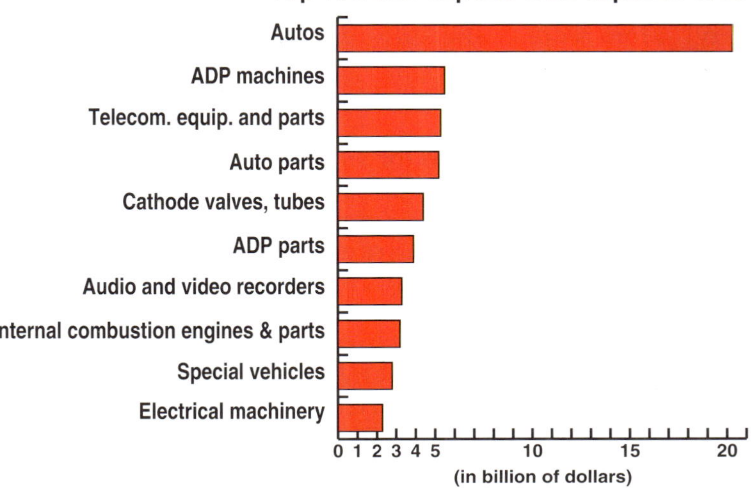

"We still make dolls, soy sauce and other traditional goods. But we also have some of the most modern factories for making computer products, cars, cameras and robots," he explained.

As we entered the assembly plant the workers all stopped and began to sing. Mr. Adachi explained: "A company song is very symbolic. Each worker is encouraged to feel that he or she is a part of a team. Many workers take part in after-hours and weekend company activities to strengthen this feeling of teamwork. They still work ten to twelve hours a day, five and one-half or six days a week. These companies offer their workers lifetime employment. Sometimes workers have to move and do different work but they are guaranteed jobs."

The bank building where Mrs. Adachi worked was one of the tallest in the area. She waved as she came out. "I must have received hundreds of *MEISHI* (*may•ee•she* - business cards) today," she said. "Everybody in Tokyo wants a loan to start or invest in a new company!"

"One hundred out of every five hundred *yen* we earn is saved," Mr. Adachi said to Dad.

Mrs. Adachi interrupted: "My biggest client is opening a new office in Sapporo. More and more of the Japanese people want to travel to Hokkaido to escape the summer heat."

INDUSTRIAL POLLUTION IN JAPAN

The side effects of industrialization are sometimes harmful, and not always predictable. In the 1960s a chemical factory near Minamata Bay discharged waste water, called **effluent**, into the sea. The effluent contained mercury. At the time, nobody realized that the mercury in the water was accidentally being converted to methyl mercury, a deadly compound which can cause numbness, paralysis, and even death.

Through the **food chain** the methyl mercury became concentrated in the fish and shellfish in the Bay.

The people living in communities around Minamata Bay mainly ate seafood from the Bay, and after a while they started to have severe health problems. It is estimated that about 700 people died and 9000 more were permanently crippled by mercury poisoning.

After the origin of the illness was found, warnings were issued about the hazard of mercury poisoning. The illnesses resulting from mercury poisoning have been given the name Minamata Disease.

"I can certainly understand why they think that way!" Mom said as she suffered through the heat of the day.

"Where are we going for supper, Goro?" Mrs. Adachi asked.

"I thought we would go for *sukiyaki* at the Tsukiji Suehiro Restaurant, just off Ginza."

"Excellent!" replied Mrs. Adachi.

As we entered the restaurant we took off our shoes. Mrs. Adachi was wearing white *TABI* (*tab•ee* - socks) on her feet.

"The owner of Tsukiji Suehiro Restaurant has kept everything as much like *Edo* as possible," Mr. Adachi explained. "There are two changes that I think you will like. The first is that you do not have to cross your legs to sit at the low table. There is a space cut out underneath the table for your legs. The second change is that the cook stove is fueled with gas rather than charcoal. This allows for better cooking and less smoke."

The lady who served us our drinks also cooked our meal right at the table. Kenny imitated his father by pouring Coke Light into my glass. I imitated Mrs. Adachi by filling Kenny's glass. Mrs. Adachi said to Mom: "It is an old **custom** to serve *sake* to your guests."

"Another example of a kind of gift giving," I said.

Mr. Adachi smiled. "I believe Lorraine is ready to understand the Tea Ceremony," he said.

JAPAN'S LABOR FORCE

Immediately following the Meiji Restoration 90% of the population worked in the primary industries. Today, only 10% of the labor force is involved in the **primary industries**; **secondary industries** account for some 31% of the labor force; and 55% are involved in the **tertiary industries**.

Although the concept of lifetime employment is still a valued tradition in Japan, workers are leaving their jobs for new opportunities. At one time it would have been a disgrace for an employee to leave his company. In this modern era, the new workers are also beginning to ask for salaries based upon abilities rather than seniority.

Modern transportation, communication, and a very high standard of living have brought the Japanese worker in constant contact with the rest of the world. These workers must choose daily whether to walk the traditional road or to leap into the twenty-first century. Current indications are that they intend in many ways to travel both roads, but if pressed, they will take the modern road into the future.

We ate with *hashi*. It was easier by now because everything was cut into bite size pieces and cooked. At the beginning and end of the meal we were given a hot towel to wipe our hands.

As we left the restaurant Dad told Mr. Adachi that the service was excellent.

Japan exports many traditional products.

Most of Japan's exports are modern goods.

Mr. Adachi agreed. "When fifty percent of your people earn their living in the service industry the quality had better be good!" he said.

"We're almost at your home!" I said. "I can't wait to meet your *obaasan*."

"You know, I haven't seen her in over a year!" said Kenny in an excited voice. "I'm looking forward to seeing her too!"

We took off our shoes in the front entrance to the house.

"It is here at the *GENKEN* (*gen•kehn* - porch) that we leave the western world outside. We change from *GETA* (*gay•tah* - outside shoes) to *ZORI* (*zoe•ree* - inside slippers)." Just as I was taking off my shoes the *shoji* slid open. A small Japanese lady bowed low and said: "*KONBAN WA*! (*kohn•bahn•wa* - good evening) *OAGARI KUDASAI*." (*Oh•a•gah•ree coo•dah•sigh* - please step up.) Kenny ran in and hugged his *obaasan*.

Mrs. Adachi indicated that she wanted us to enter the house. It was during the introductions that I was surprised. Kenny's *obaasan* started by saying in *Eigo,* "Welcome to our home. I am sorry it is so small but we will try to offer you something satisfactory."

Obaasan saw my puzzled face. "I studied English at the same time that Kenny did," she said. "We *Nihonjin* have a long history of knowing which traditions to keep and which ways of other people to learn. Besides, it gave me something useful to do. My father, Kenny's great-grandfather, was a farmer. He often took me to a market where *Eigo* was spoken by the buyers," she continued.

I couldn't believe how well she spoke *Eigo* and how young she looked. Kenny had told me that she was almost seventy years old, but she barely looked fifty.

"We are very pleased to meet you! We want to thank you for allowing us to visit!" Mom said.

Mr. Adachi had offered to show Dad the outside. When they returned Dad said that there were a patio deck and a beautiful **terraced** garden. The roof was tile shingles made of clay and the walls were made of cement. There were trees everywhere you looked!

Inside we saw a small kitchen with lots of modern appliances, and a Western-style dining table with four regular chairs. *Obaasan* showed me a modern electric **rice cooker**. "I still have to wash the rice kernels and measure one cup of

water for each cup of rice but I don't have to time the steaming period. It is so nice to be able to just push a button," she said.

Mrs. Adachi added: "*Obaasan*, remember that when you make *sushi* you still prefer to use the cast iron cooker."

"Special things deserve the time and care of the old ways," *Obaasan* replied. "Many times the care and effort in making something means that it will be valued more. It is good to be interested in more than just the finished product."

The main room, which Kenny called a *CHANOMA* (*cha•noh•mah* - main room of the house), had a color television, stereo system and a *KOTASU* (*koe•tah•soo* - low table) with an electric grill in the middle of it. There were small square pillows on the floor around the *kotasu*.

Kenny showed me his room. It had a desk and a computer, a bed, a T.V. and a stereo. Everything was so neat and tidy.

The main bathroom in the Adachi house had a large tub and a washing area beside the *OFURO* (*oh•fuu•roh* - tub). The toilet was in a separate room and had a basin for washing your hands. Special *zori* were outside the door to the toilet.

Mrs. Adachi and Kenny's *obaasan* showed us the *BUTSUDAN* (*boot•sue•dahn* - family altar). A picture of Kenny's *ojiisan* was on the shelf. There was a place for incense sticks beside a bowl of fresh fruit. Mrs. Adachi had also placed a flower arrangement in a crystal vase beside the picture. Mrs. Adachi said proudly that the *IKEBANA* (*ee•kay•bah•na* - flower arrangement) was the result of taking lessons for ten Saturdays.

Obaasan showed us the master bedroom. "Goro has gone soft and bought a waterbed!" she said. "I still prefer to sleep on a *FUTON* (*foo•tohn* - sleeping mattress) in the main room. Every day I hang the *futon* outside. The summer air in *Nihon* is very damp and the *futons* must be dried each day."

In another room the floor was covered in *TATAMI* (*tah•tah•mee* - mats made of rice straw). "These mats are made of woven rice straw, hemp and cotton," explained Mrs. Adachi.

"You have a real Van Gogh!" Mom interrupted.

Mrs. Adachi blushed. "My father, Kenny's *ojiisan*, was given that when he retired from the bank as its longest serving manager. When you visit Sapporo you will see one of the finest collections of European artists anywhere."

Obaasan interrupted: "We should explain the Tea Ceremony so that we can get on our way! We do not want to be late!

"The *CHADO* (*chah•doh* - Tea Ceremony) is a way of

Exterior of a Japanese house.

Interior of a Japanese house.

showing high class and status in *Nihon*. It is performed by one person for one or more guests. Usually a separate tea house is built in a garden and is only used for the *Chado.* In the *Chado*, the position of the utensils, the way of holding the cups, the mixing of the ingredients, and the sharing of the tea is what is important. The goal is to show that one is skilled and willing to take the time to perform the ceremony in a perfect way," explained *Obaasan*.

"A gift from one person to another!" I said.

"Careful, Lorraine!" said Mr. Adachi, "I think your blond hair is beginning to turn black!"

"He means you are becoming smart in the ways of the *Nihonjin*!" laughed Kenny.

As we walked down the dark alley towards the Matsubaya Tea House in Asakusa, I again felt like we were in *Edo*. Every once in a while we could hear the clicking and clopping that *Obaasan* said was the *geta* of the *geisha*s.

We arrived at the large wooden building with ceramic tiles on the roof. It was a strange place for such an old building. Highrises were on both sides of the tea house. We entered through a wooden gate. The stone path took us through a Japanese rock garden. "This garden is an attempt to show or capture our closeness to nature," Mr. Adachi explained. "The running waterfalls represent rivers; the rocks are the mountains; the trees are forests, and the ponds are oceans." When we came to the *genken,* a lady slid open the *shoji.*

Kenny showed me the *BONSAI* (bon•sai - dwarf tree) on a shelf. "The *Nihonjin* have been raising miniature potted pine trees for over a thousand years!" he said.

"A *bonsai* is carefully shaped by cutting small branches and sometimes using wires to bring other branches closer together," Mrs. Adachi added.

"I remember," I said, "in the movie *The Karate Kid* the old man said to see it in his mind like a picture and then re-create it!"

A Japanese bonsai tree.

"Even in *Edo* you manage to refer to modern things, Lorraine!" Mr. Adachi said with a laugh. "There is one thing about the film that is very true. The people of Okinawa use the art of sculpting *bonsai* for relaxing, **meditation** and coming closer to nature."

The lady asked us to take off our *geta* and to change into *zori*. We were seated on *tatami*. The lady asked if we would like something to drink. We all chose *ocha*.

A man dressed in a white *kimono* came out and welcomed us. He knew Mr. Adachi: "*Konban wa* Adachi-SAN! (*sahn* - sir or madam, a suffix of respect) *OGENKI DESU KA*?" (*Oh•gen•kee day•su•ka* - how are you?) Mr. Adachi smiled, bowed and introduced us to Mr. Kadonaga. The evening's entertainment and service was being provided by *OIRAN* (*oh•ee•ran* - elite) *geisha*s. These ladies were from thirty to fifty years old; the younger women were the **apprentices** or *MAIKO* (*mah•ee•koh* - apprentice geishas) and learning to be *geisha*s.

"The *geisha*s have been in training since they were your age!" commented Mrs. Adachi. "They have studied under very skilled artists. Each *geisha* is a talented singer, dancer, actress and musician. Tonight they will *BUYO,* (*boo•yoe* - dance) sing, and play the *shamisen* and the *koto*."

"If Mr. Kuilboer is willing they will also demonstrate the Tea Ceremony to him," explained Mr. Kadonaga.

We all encouraged Dad to be a good sport. I've never seen him blush so much. He finally agreed, after much laughing and kidding.

"As soon as we have Kuilboer-*san* properly dressed we will begin your evening in *Edo*," Mr. Kadonaga said.

When Dad was brought out by the two *geisha* ladies he was dressed in a traditional *kimono*. The two ladies with him were dressed in very bright *kimonos*, had their hair in a fancy style and had white faces with striking make-up.

A man began to play the *TAIKO* (*tie•koh* - drum) and Mr. Kadonaga explained that the dances represent the special regions or KEN (*koen* - regions) of *Nihon*.

After much singing and dancing the *Chado* was performed for Dad. Mr. Kadonaga explained the importance of the special china and instruments being used. Everything had been crafted by hand. The *geisha* moved in a way that resembled a slow motion figure skater or dancer.

"Tonight you have truly travelled the road to *Edo*," *Obaasan* said.

"I am sure," Mrs. Adachi said, "that you will enjoy the rest of your trip. Each of Japan's regions are like the different regions of the United States."

"*Nihon* is like home in so many ways," I said. "But in the United States people keep customs from many countries including *Nihon*. Here in *Nihon*, whatever is borrowed or kept from other countries is somehow made Japanese."

"You will always find some things that are, in a special way, only Japanese!" Kenny said.

"Goro and I would like to join you but we must go to work, "Mrs. Adachi said. "Kenny is very lucky. He will be able to see the old and new *Nihon* through your eyes."

"It's the old road for me!" I said.

Dad came out from behind a curtain. "For me too! You know, Alice, I think you should become a *maiko* and take lessons from the *geisha*s!" We all laughed.

"Ted, you know a *maiko* must begin training as a teenager," Mom said. "Besides, I'm sure you enjoy being waited on more than you did the entertainment!"

Mom then winked and we all laughed again. Mr. Adachi also reminded Dad that in the old days of *Edo* everyone walked from one part of the country to the other. There were no roads or super expressways, just foot paths and bridges across the many streams. The countryside was too rough for dirt roads and there were too many earthquakes for stone roads. "The old way was good but there are some real advantages to modern *Nihon*," he concluded.

Mr. Kadonaga walked with us as we returned to our car. He wished us well and thanked Mr. Adachi for the pleasure of serving us. Everyone took turns bowing.

Japanese women are assuming modern roles.

We said goodnight and were on our way home.

I asked Mrs. Adachi: "Are the women of *Nihon* happy in their role? Japanese men seem to be **chauvinistic**."

"Now Yoshi, be careful what you say about me!" Mr. Adachi said, but he had a big smile on his face.

Mom said what I was thinking. "Goro called you 'Yoshi'. I am puzzled."

"Goro calls me Yoshi, my first name, when we are talking about my work, or the western ideas of a working woman's role," Mrs. Adachi explained. "Fumiko is my middle name and the one used by *Obaasan*, Goro and Kenny most of the time, especially at home. Even though I like to work outside of our house, I am also very proud of my ability to run a good home."

"It took a long time for me to accept this idea," *Obaasan* added. "I kept telling Fumiko that she had more than enough to do at home. I also complained that she was making me do most things. I was wrong."

"Many Japanese men, including Goro, often consider certain things 'women's work'," Mrs. Adachi continued. "But all of those things are also done by men. Men in *Nihon* learn to *buyo*, sing, act, wash, cook, and do *ikebana*. *Obaasan* is teaching Kenny the *Chado*. There are very few things that a man does that are seen by others as being unmanly."

"Women doing the same job as men in *Nihon* get paid less and are treated with less respect by their bosses, who usually are men," added Mr. Adachi. "It is wrong, I don't agree with it, but that is the way it is in both *Nihon* and the United States."

"It is confusing," Kenny said. "I think that in some ways women in *Nihon* are better off than in the United States and in other ways it is worse. Mom handles all of our family's money. Dad and Mom always decide what we are going to do together."

"Thanks, Kenny," Mr. Adachi said, "but don't forget that when you were very young I often stayed out late with my friends from work."

"Goro would often finish work at 10:00 P.M., go out for two or three hours and then take the subway home," Mrs. Adachi explained. "He would often go to sleep at 2:00 A.M. and get up at 6:00 A.M. for work. I had to run the house or it would not get done."

Mr. Adachi protested with a laugh. "But I have changed. I do my share of the cooking and cleaning. Now, it is Yoshi who is often late coming home."

"And Goro does housework very well!" *Obaasan* said.

Mr. Adachi replied: "Thanks, *Okaasan*!"

We all laughed.

"Lorraine, you will soon be leaving to see the rest of *Nihon*," Mrs. Adachi added. "Along the way you will see women behaving in very traditional and modern ways."

I went to sleep dreaming of being a *geisha* and then of making big decisions in my corporate office in one of Tokyo's highrise office towers.

Tomorrow we are leaving to travel another road.

Chapter 6

OFF THE BEATEN TRACK

JAPANESE VOCABULARY

WORDS

Ainu	ah•ee•nuu	Aborigines of Hokkaido
denwa	den•wah	telephone
iro	ee•roh	color
kiiroi	kee•doy	yellow
kohii	koh•hee	coffee
miso	mee•soh	soup
sensei	sen•say	teacher
takushii	tah•koo•shee	taxi

PHRASES and SENTENCES

Hai! Ii desu ne!	hie ee day•su neh	Yes! Great!
Ii desu ne!	ee day•su neh	Great!
Nihongo ga sukoshi shika hanasemasen.	Nee•hon•go ga skosh•ee shee•kah hah•nah• say•mah•sen	I speak a little Japanese too.

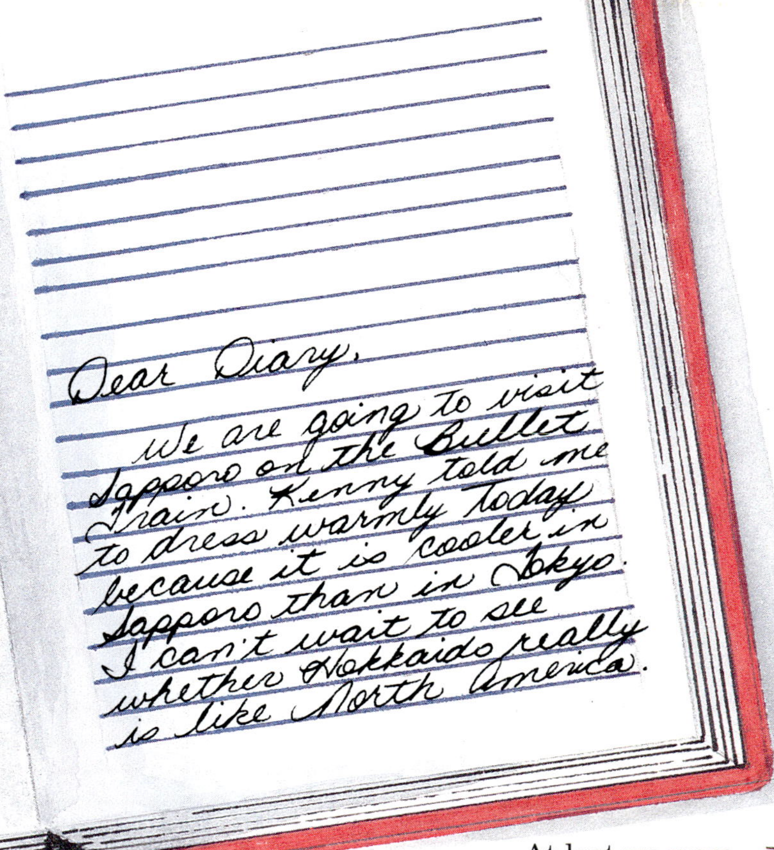
Dear Diary,
We are going to visit Sapporo on the Bullet Train. Kenny told me to dress warmly today because it is cooler in Sapporo than in Tokyo. I can't wait to see whether Hokkaido really is like North America.

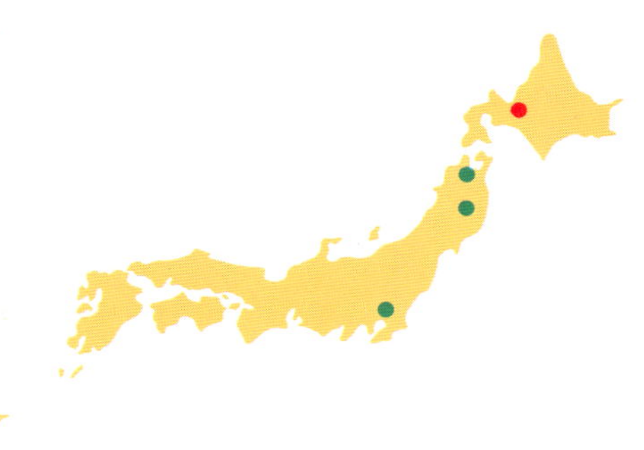

Looking out the window, I noticed that great care had been taken to plant trees in industrial areas. Highrises exist next to *Shinto* shrines and burial grounds. People in homes that have stereos and televisions hang the wash out to dry each day.

"Though this city produces millions of cars, has rapid transit, subways, and so many taxis, the most common types of transportation are bicycling and walking," I said in amazement to Kenny.

At last we were about to discover the northern part of *Nihon*. Kenny and I went down to the track area where I got my first close-up look at the Shinkansen. "It looks like it's built for space travel," I said.

"Wait until you discover why it's nicknamed the bullet train," Kenny replied.

As we stood on the platform and looked in the windows of the train we could see the cleaning crew quickly moving through the train. The seats were swivelled to face the opposite direction and the head rest covers were replaced with new white cloths.

The train began to leave the station and a tape-recorded voice said: "Ladies and gentlemen: Welcome aboard the Tohoku Shinkansen."

Kenny proudly stated: "The name of our train is the Yamabiko. Other bullet trains called the Tokaido and the Sanyo Shinkansen trains leave from Tokyo station for southern *Nihon*. When we go to Kyoto we will take the train called Hikari."

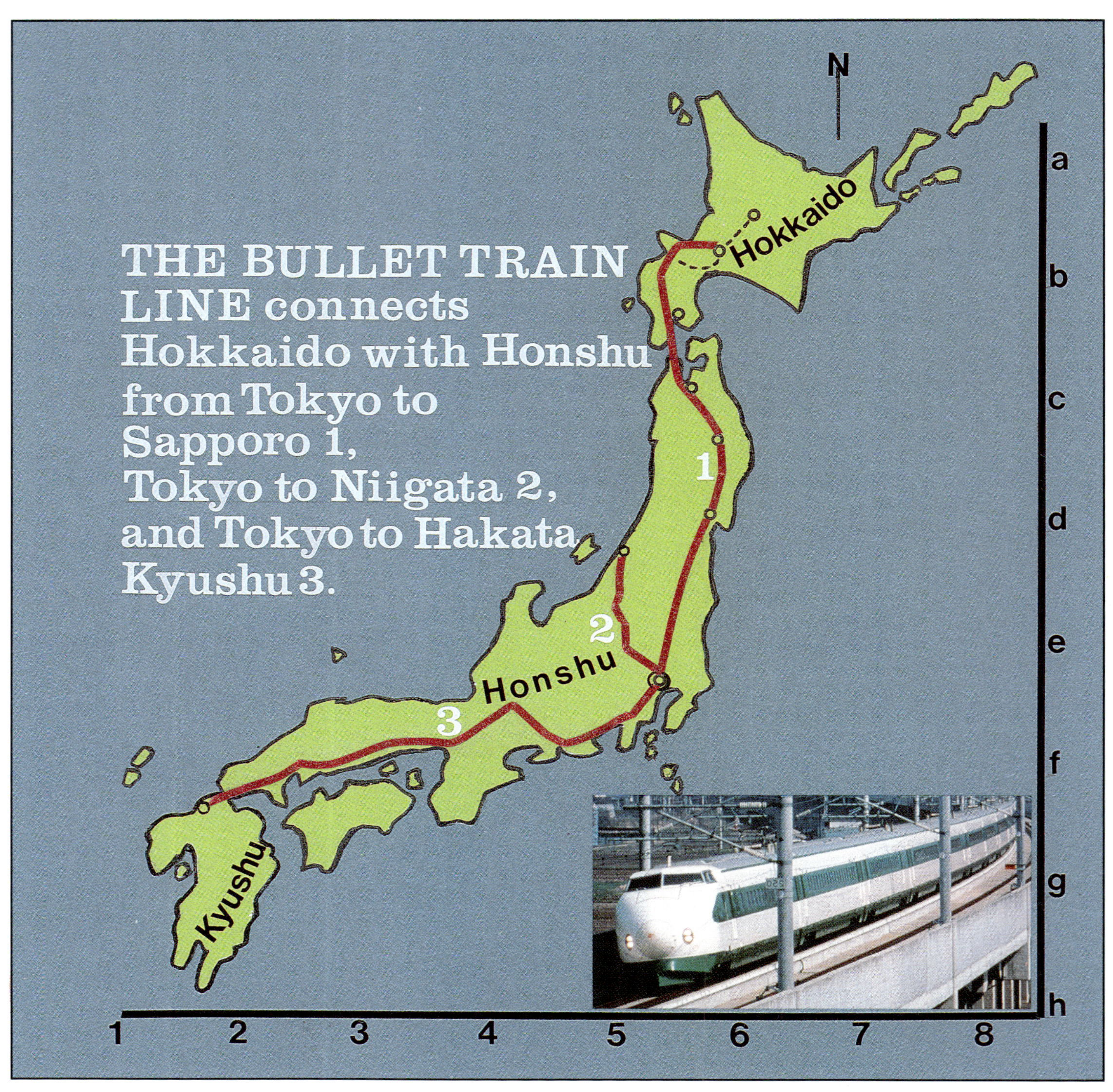
THE BULLET TRAIN LINE connects Hokkaido with Honshu from Tokyo to Sapporo 1, Tokyo to Niigata 2, and Tokyo to Hakata Kyushu 3.
N
Hokkaido
Honshu
Kyushu
1
2
3
a
b
c
d
e
f
g
h
1
2
3
4
5
6
7
8

"You must remember that it is very difficult to find a place to park a car. One of the costs of rapid growth and **industrialization** in *Nihon* has been severe overcrowding," explained Kenny.

As we continued north the train shifted into high gear. According to the digital speedometer at the front of our car, we were now travelling at 240 kilometers per hour. The land to the west was rising into hills and mountains. "The haze is lifting and the sky is blue!" Kenny observed.

"Everything is so green. It's like a big garden," I said.

"It is nice to see a clear sky. The Japanese have done much to clean up the pollution caused by industry. But it is only in the countryside that the really clear skies exist," Dad said to Mom.

Japanese countryside as seen from the bullet train.

INDUSTRIALIZATION

Following World War II, Japan rapidly became an industrialized country. Problems with labor unrest, housing shortages, transportation bottlenecks, and pollution accompanied this rapid growth. However, these problems have been or are being addressed.

Japan's gross national product is among the highest in the world. The four main Japanese industrial areas of Keihin, Chukyo, Hanshin, and Kita-Kyuhu have grown steadily. Increased overseas trade and initiatives to have the population increase their purchases of local goods are effectively limiting the threat of unemployment in Japan.

"It must have been awful during the 1960s to have had to worry about the air you breathed," Mom replied.

"At the time it was simply one of the costs of industrialization," Dad replied.

On our trip we went through small towns like ***Omiya*** and ***Fukushima***. The landscape flashed by as we sped toward Morioka.

"This train is very fast but smooth," I said. "You can't really tell by just sitting here that we are even moving but whenever I try to take a picture of something it is gone before I can press the shutter."

"Just have a little **patience** Lorraine," Mom said, "and you will see many things worthy of a picture."

"All I know is that I'm glad this camera is automatic! I shot lots of pictures of people working in the rice fields. I hope they turn out!" I answered.

I thought about Mom's word – patience. Mrs. Adachi had told me that the *Nihonjin* valued patience in everything they do. I was confused. These people move at an extremely fast pace and yet there is always time to be polite. Even when they are crowding onto trains, subways and elevators they are, in their own way, patient and polite. I guess this is why they employ "people pushers" to help people get on the train.

There are many things in *Nihon* that can lead to confusion. This is a land that **values** cleanliness and yet the walls and floors of public washrooms might be left dirty. In the same area, people will be outside their shops sweeping the sidewalks clean.

Kenny brought me back from my private thinking. "That little boy across the way is staring at you."

I turned and saw a small round face looking over the back of a seat. The little boy was standing on the lap of an elderly Japanese man. A younger man, probably in his thirties, was seated next to them.

"In *Nihon* the elderly are respected and the children are often spoiled," I said to Kenny.

Mom interrupted: "I think the children are valued more than they are spoiled. They certainly are always well behaved."

"Children are always well cared for and given lots of attention," Kenny said. "You must remember that the eldest son has the duty to provide for the well-being of his parents."

"That is why Mr. Adachi takes such great care in seeing to the needs of his obaasan," said Dad. "The dignity of the elderly means everything to the *Nihonjin*."

Kenny continued. "My *ojiisan* once told me that the *Nihonjin* want to have the best in this life and the best in the next life. We are very practical when it comes to deciding between traditions and new ways of doing things. **Face**, or dignity, is very important."

"We should be in Morioka in two minutes and thirteen seconds," Dad announced.

We laughed at Dad's faith in Mr. Adachi's statement that the train would be on time. Then we were shocked when Dad announced that it was exactly 11:25 A.M. and two minutes later the doors of the train opened for us.

Skiing is a very popular sport in Japan.

Sapporo hosted the 1972 Winter Olympics.

As we walked around Morioka we saw several people who were preparing for a summer festival. Festivals are celebrated throughout the year but the summer is a really busy time.

Everywhere we went little children kept staring at me. "Some of these children have never seen anyone with blond hair like yours," Kenny said.

"In *Nihon*, Morioka is the starting point for skiing," Kenny said. "We have travelled far enough north for snow to fall in the mountains during the winter."

"It is much cooler here," I replied. "I am so glad to be away from the heat of Tokyo."

"Look at the snow suits!" Mom pointed out.

I liked the bright colors worn by the Japanese skiers. "There seems to be lots of snow and the ski hills are quite large," added Dad.

"Look, there's an advertisement for a Pro-Am race like the ones we have at home!" I exclaimed.

"I remember how surprised we were that your family already knew how to ski," Dad said to Kenny.

"It's one more thing that we have borrowed that I really like," replied Kenny. "Did you know that *Nihon* hosted the Winter Olympics in Sapporo in 1972? Japanese are very interested in skiing but we are learning other winter sports too," said Kenny. "*Nihon* now has a national hockey team."

"I guess that is another thing that has been adopted from North America," I said proudly.

The next morning, after a breakfast of *MISO* (*mee•soh*-soup), fish, rice, and *KOHII* (*koh•hee*-coffee), we took a *TAKUSHII* (*tah•koo•shee*-taxi) to the station.

"We will arrive in Aomori at 11:57 A.M.," Kenny said.

"This *densha* from Moroika to Aomori is not as fast as the Shinkansen but we will still get there in just over two hours," I said.

Mom was talking to a man in the next seat. She introduced us. "Lorraine and Kenny, this is Mr. Carlylle Whitelaw. Mr. Whitelaw, this is my daughter Lorraine and her friend, Kenny Adachi. Mr. Whitelaw is from Toronto, Canada."

Japan now has a national hockey team.

"I'm pleased to meet you Lorraine. *Konnichi wa*, Kenny," Mr. Whitelaw said.

"*Ohayo Gozaimasu*!" Kenny answered.

"Lorraine speaks and understands a little Japanese too," Mom added.

I tried to say in my very best *Nihongo*: "*NIHONGO GA SUKOSHI SHIKA HANASEMASEN*" (*nee•hon•go ga skosh•ee shee•kah hah•nah•say•mah•sen*- I speak a little Japanese too).

"*II DESU NE*! " (*ee day•su neh*-great!) Mr. Whitelaw said. "You both speak *Nihongo* and *Eigo* very well."

"Lorraine's a good student and I spent the past year in California," Kenny said. "Where did you learn to speak *Nihongo*, Mr. Whitelaw?"

"I have been teaching at Kobe University for the past two years. I also visit a friend of mine once each year to help with a High School English class in Sapporo."

It was a very interesting trip. The countryside was really beautiful. The farms are kept like flower gardens. We noticed that there were many signs of modern *Nihon* right alongside the traditional things.

We only had ten minutes to get off the train and onto the ferry to Hokkaido. We had just sat down when the ferry began to move. "Let's go out on deck so we can see the Island and the ***Tsugaru Strait***," I said.

"Put on your jacket. We are heading north and the ocean breeze will be cool," Mom said.

Only four hours after we had left Aomori, we arrived in Hokadate and boarded the Lex Hokuto Express Train for Sapporo. I noticed right away that Hokkaido is like parts of our western states.

"There are many similarities between Hokkaido and the mountain areas in the western United States," Kenny said.

"Ted, look at the pine trees, the thick vegetation, the ranches. There's even a log home!" exclaimed Mom.

JAPAN'S CLIMATE

Japan's climate is relatively mild with distinct seasons. In early summer there is a rainy season. **Typhoons** begin in the summer and reach their peak in September and October. Flooding and landslides are common during the typhoon season. Hot and humid southeasterly **monsoons** blow in from the Pacific Ocean in the summer. In contrast, cold northwesterly monsoons bring winter in from China.

Japan is a long narrow country stretching from north to south, therefore, the weather varies greatly during any season from region to region. For example, Okinawa will remain relatively warm (16°C) even in January while winter temperatures drop to between -5°C and -10°C in the north. Summer temperatures may range from 19°C in Hokkaido to above 30°C in Tokyo.

The Pacific coast receives high amounts of summer rainfall, while the Japan Sea coast receives heavy winter snows. The inland areas generally receive less rainfall than the coasts, and the southwest islands remain warm all year round.

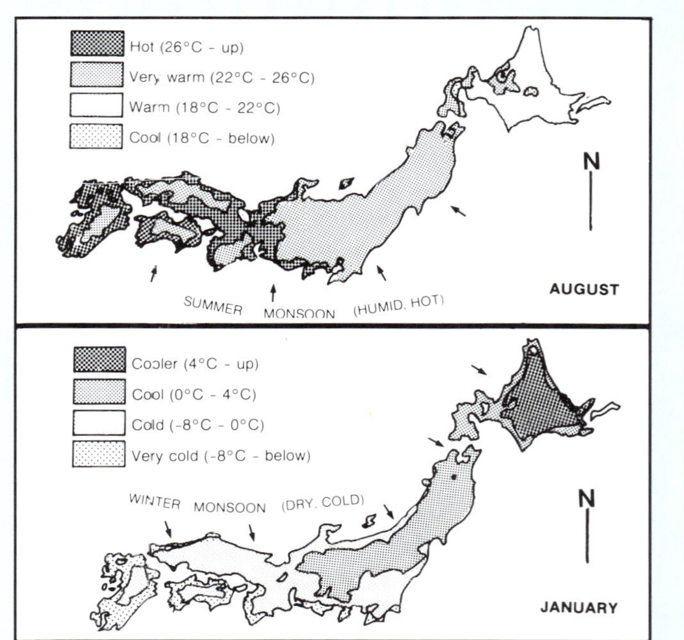

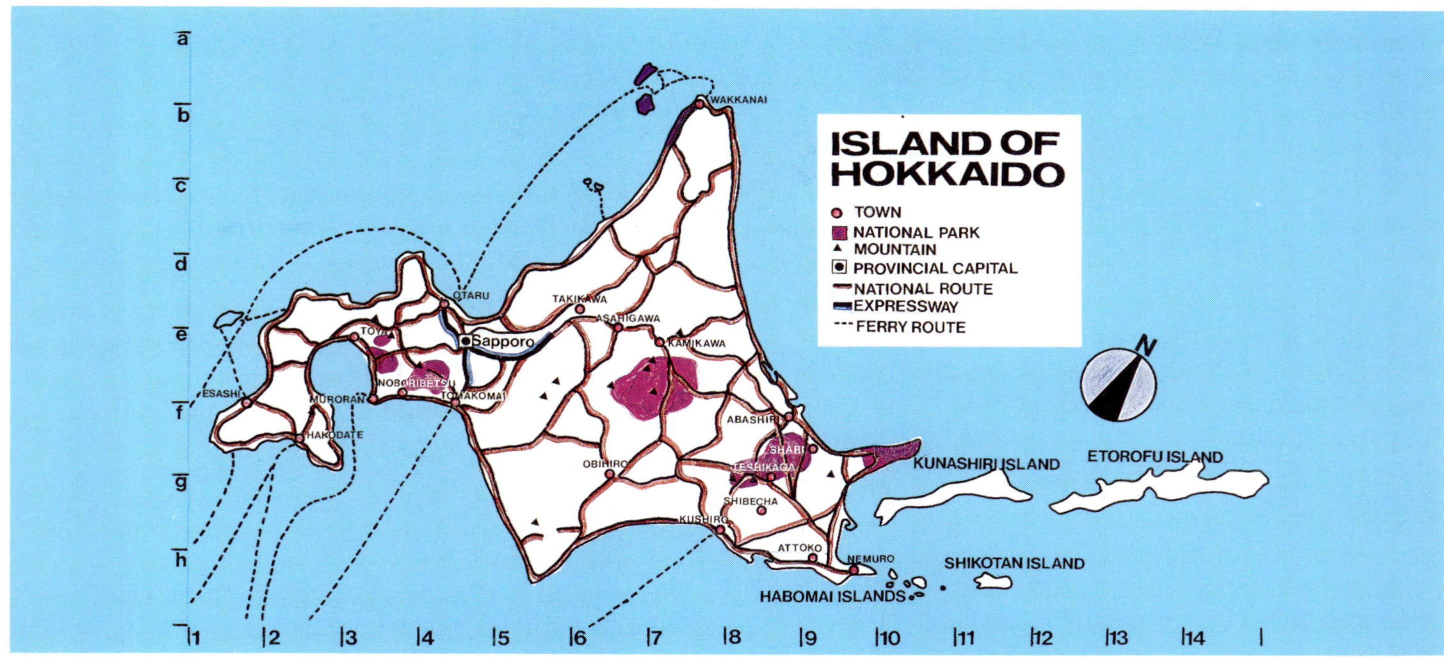

"I'll bet that is one of the log homes that is made in North America, and exported to *Nihon*," said Dad with confidence.

"Oh, look at the large modern houses," Mom continued. "This really does look like home."

Dad explained that the Japanese build railway tunnels along the coast through the mountains in straight lines. This ensures that the tunnel is perfectly level. The trains reach some of their highest speeds in these tunnels. The countryside went by very quickly. The variety of landscape and scenery was impressive.

"Lorraine, you write down all the different things that I call out," said Kenny, "and we'll make a list of things we see in Hokkaido and then we can check if any of them exist in other parts of *Nihon*."

"Okay, I'm ready," I replied.

"Grain elevator, barns, cows, combine, tractor," shouted Kenny.

"Thank goodness we are going into another tunnel and you can't see anything. I can't write that fast!" I protested.

"Pine trees, ocean, mountains, snow, wave barriers, fishing boats, nets, houses, rice fields, another train, cars, trucks, bicycles–," Kenny continued.

"Stop! Stop! My fingers are falling off!" I shouted in frustration. "I want to look at all of these things you are listing off too!"

I could see the ocean and the mountains at the same time. Everything was green. The sky was blue not grey. There was so much open space.

"Are the trains in Hokkaido always this full?" Mom asked Kenny.

"The Japanese are their own best tourists," Kenny replied. "Japanese from southern *Nihon* come to see the scenery and to escape the summer heat. They also come to see the countryside.

"Hokkaido," Kenny continued, "was settled with some help from American advisors. That is why the agriculture and the buildings look so much like those in North America. In Sapporo the museums carry the whole story of this settlement activity."

"Hokkaido is a lot like the United States. The stores even have stuffed or wooden bears and foxes as their tourist symbols. It's a lot like Yosemite!" I said.

We went to ***Odori Park***. It is a long narrow park in the middle of Sapporo. Streets run on both sides of this park. We went up the ***Television Tower***. From the top of the tower we could see the ski jumping site that had been used when Sapporo was the host city for the 1972 Olympic Winter Games.

When we left the park we went to the ***Hokkaido Prefecture Government Grounds***. Mom described the gardens as the most beautiful and peaceful place she had ever seen. Dad was taking pictures as fast as his camera would allow him to.

"I'm already on my sixth roll of film. We'll have to stop and get more," he stated.

Kenny and I wandered around the paths that were beside the ponds. We came upon an elderly man who explained to Kenny, in *Nihongo*, about the ducks. He said that he had to wear the right shirt in order for the ducks to come to feed out of his hand.

"How could you understand everything that he said and translate it so quickly?" I asked Kenny. "I could only understand one or two words."

AGRICULTURE IN JAPAN

Since the end of World War II, the manufacturing industries have replaced agriculture as the most important part of Japan's economy. Formerly a country that lived off the products of farming and fishing, Japan now relies heavily on imported foods. Farmers once accounted for 50% of the population and now account for a mere 8%.

The Japanese government acknowledges that a lot of good farm land is being paved over by the concrete of the sprawling cities. Where land remains fertile, paddy-field rice cultivation is widespread. Each year more and more of the land is transferred to the growing of vegetables and fruits. In the North, increasing amounts of land are being dedicated to the raising of cattle. This is a result of the increasing popularity of milk and beef as supplements to the traditionally fish-based Japanese diet.

Mechanization and irrigation have not had a great effect on the productivity of the farm lands. However, the use of fertilizer has helped the farming industry. Along with these changes, the farm home has also changed. Farm homes today are, for the most part, more modern and spacious than those found in the cities.

Even busy executives enjoy the beauty of Nakajima Park.

"He spoke the same dialect as my father," explained Kenny. "He used to live in ***Tottori-ken*** before he moved to Sapporo. You will remember that that is where my great-grandfather lived," he continued.

"Before we came here I just thought that all Japanese people would speak *Nihongo* the same way," Dad said. "Now that I think about it I feel foolish. This is a country with many distinct **regions**."

"The people in the south did not mix with the people in the north until recent times," added Kenny.

We found out that that Hokkaido had been inhabited since ancient times by the *AINU* (*ah•ee•nuu* - Aborigines of Hokkaido) and that most Japanese considered Hokkaido simply to be an island of snow and ice. As time went by and the people of *Nihon* travelled more, most of the *Ainu* were mixed into the group that we know today as Japanese.

"I have read that Hokkaido was colonized and settled much like the Big Island in Hawaii," Mom said. "Ranches and railways have been influenced by North American cattle barons and engineers."

We went to an area called ***Susukino*** where there were lots of neon lights, nightclubs, fashion stores, and gift shops. Afterwards, we used the *DENWA* (*den•wah* - telephone) to call Kenny's parents.

Denwa in *Nihon* are different than phones in the United States. The phones for different areas are marked by *IRO* (*ee•roh* - color). We used a *KIIROI* (*kee•doy* - yellow) *denwa* to call Tokyo.

Mrs. Adachi said that she wished she could be with us. She said, "It sounds like you are having a lot of fun! I hope you are enjoying the weather. It is too hot to do much but sweat here in Tokyo."

We visited the Botanical Gardens. Mom fell in love with all of the pretty flowers. Dad must have taken hundreds of snapshots. Even Kenny took lots of photographs. We then went to ***Nakajima Park.*** I noticed some ladies painting landscapes. Others were taking a lesson from a man in a blue smock.

Kenny took us to the Japanese garden in the park. We just sat there and enjoyed the peaceful setting of the garden. No one even felt the need to talk.

I noticed a businessman walk briskly into the park. He suddenly stopped and simply watched the children feeding the ducks and fish.

"Even the busiest executive has time to enjoy the beauty of nature and people in *Nihon*," I heard Dad tell Mom.

The next morning we were up early to get ready to leave Sapporo. It was hard to believe that four days had passed by so quickly. When we got to the train station we had to go through tunnels under the tracks to get to the right platform.

I became separated from the others and almost got lost. I had to ask for directions. The ticket agent checked my ticket stub, and was able to point out the way. I almost missed the train.

On the Seikan Ferry to Aomori I was sitting on the sun deck trying to get a tan. Kenny pointed out the group of school girls that had travelled on the ferry when we had first come to Hokkaido. "They are on their way home after having spent the week in Hokkaido," he said. "They are asking their English teacher how to say: 'Would you have your picture taken with us?' in *Eigo*. Get ready, here they come."

I was both flattered and embarrassed when they said in unison and in perfect *Eigo*: "Would you have your picture taken with us, please?"

"*HAI II DESU NE*!" (*hie ee day•su neh* - Yes! Great!) They put me in the middle of all of them and asked Kenny to take the pictures. He didn't have to say smile or cheese. We were all laughing at how he looked like the stereotyped tourist with nine cameras strapped around his neck.

After the pictures were taken, the girls introduced us to their *SENSEI* (*sen•say* - teacher). Her name was Miss Tanaka. She told us that they were from Morioka and were on their way home from Hokadate. She explained that each year the students from her school travel to a different part of *Nihon* to study the history, geography and people of *Nihon*.

"Each region is so different from the others," Miss Tanaka said. "It is only in the last ten or twelve years that the Japanese people have begun to travel a lot in their own country and to other countries."

I asked Miss Tanaka if she had ever been to North America. "Oh, yes!" she said. "I studied at the University of California as an English major." She even knew where Beaver Creek was! I was impressed.

I asked her what she thought was the main difference between North Americans and the Japanese. "There are more similarities than there are differences," she answered. "I may be biased but I think *Nihonjin* are more willing to help and serve one another than are most North Americans. Even as we compete to be a major country in the twenty-first century we still value cooperation, caring and sharing."

We said our good-byes. Miss Tanaka promised to have her class write to my friends in Beaver Creek. She reminded me a lot of my own teacher, Mrs. Sauer.

Chapter 7

RUSHING TO THE PAST

JAPANESE VOCABULARY

WORDS

eki	**eh•kee**	**train station**

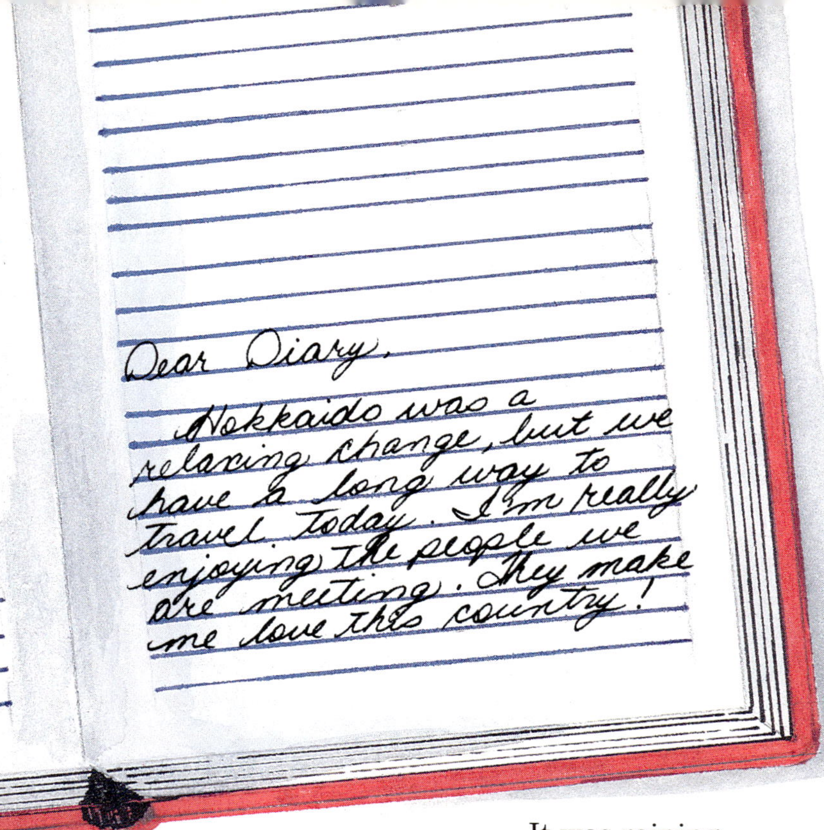

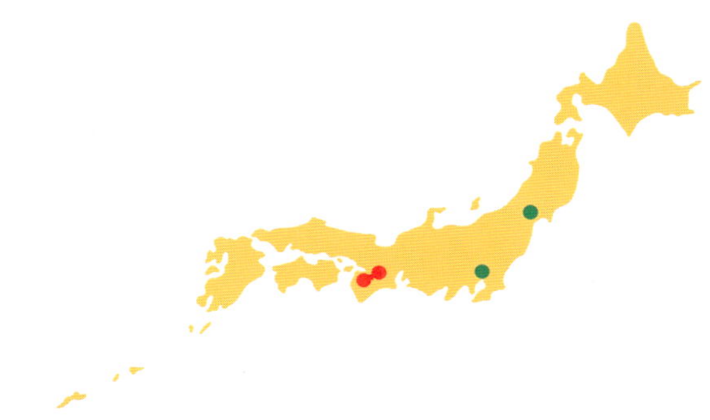

It was raining outside so we used our umbrellas. It was strange to be hot and yet feel the need to be protected from the rain. We went by taxi to the Sendai Station. Today we would go from Sendai to Ueno Station in Tokyo then to Kyoto. "Here we are!" said Kenny.

"This *EKI* (*eh-kee* - train station) is very large!" I exclaimed. "Look! There is an overhead walkway that goes to all four corners of the intersection!" I continued.

Almost all of the signs in Sendai are written in *Kanji*.

We travelled through the Japanese countryside at very fast speeds. Everything seemed to be a blur. Before we knew what was happening Kenny was saying: "We are entering Ueno Station and we have to catch the commuter train to Tokyo *Eki*. We have only forty-seven minutes to get there and catch the Hikari Shinkansen Express to Kyoto."

"We'll have to run all the way!" I protested.

We made the train just as it was pulling out of the station and had to jump on board. We had actually made all of our connections!

"You can tell this is Tokyo! You can just feel the heat!" announced Mom.

We arrived in Kyoto later that afternoon. The scenery along the way was magnificent. Every part of *Nihon* seemed different.

"Mr. Adachi said if we walked out the front doors of the train station we would see a shuttle bus standing across the street," Dad said.

"Ted, all I see are buses!" said Mom.

"Remember, Mrs. Adachi said that the front entrance is on the opposite side of the station from the buses," I reminded everybody.

"Look at all the taxis on this side of the station. It looks like the Toyota parking lot!" added Kenny.

We were loaded down with pamphlets and maps when the time came to get on the bus. In Kyoto the signs are almost all in *Nihongo*. We really had arrived in old *Nihon*.

Our bus driver was dressed in a full uniform and wore white gloves. He was very friendly and explained to Kenny that our hotel was in the suburbs of Kyoto. It was a long distance from the downtown area. Our hotel had a pool and an outdoor barbecue restaurant, but the meal prices posted on the menus were very expensive. A barbecue dinner was ¥5,000 a person! We finally went to the hotel restaurant dining room and had steak and hamburgers.

Before going to bed we called Mr. and Mrs. Adachi on the *denwa*. "One of Kyoto's famous summer festivals begins tomorrow," Mr. Adachi said. "The Gion Matsuri Festival begins with a parade. You must go downtown and see the floats!"

Mr. Adachi gave Dad the directions. While Dad was writing as fast as he could, Mom was looking at a map of the city. Mr. Adachi's last words were: "Have fun in the crowds. Hundreds of thousands of people will be joining you!"

We took the shuttle bus to Kyoto *Eki* and walked to the parade area. It was a nice fresh morning.

Mom said: "Let's just follow those people in front of us. I'm sure they are going to the parade. They certainly are dressed up for a festival."

As we got closer to the parade route we saw several men dressed in *kimonos* pulling a float on wheels. We took several pictures while we continued to walk. Everybody was laughing and singing and having a good time.

Mom found a really good spot on the parade

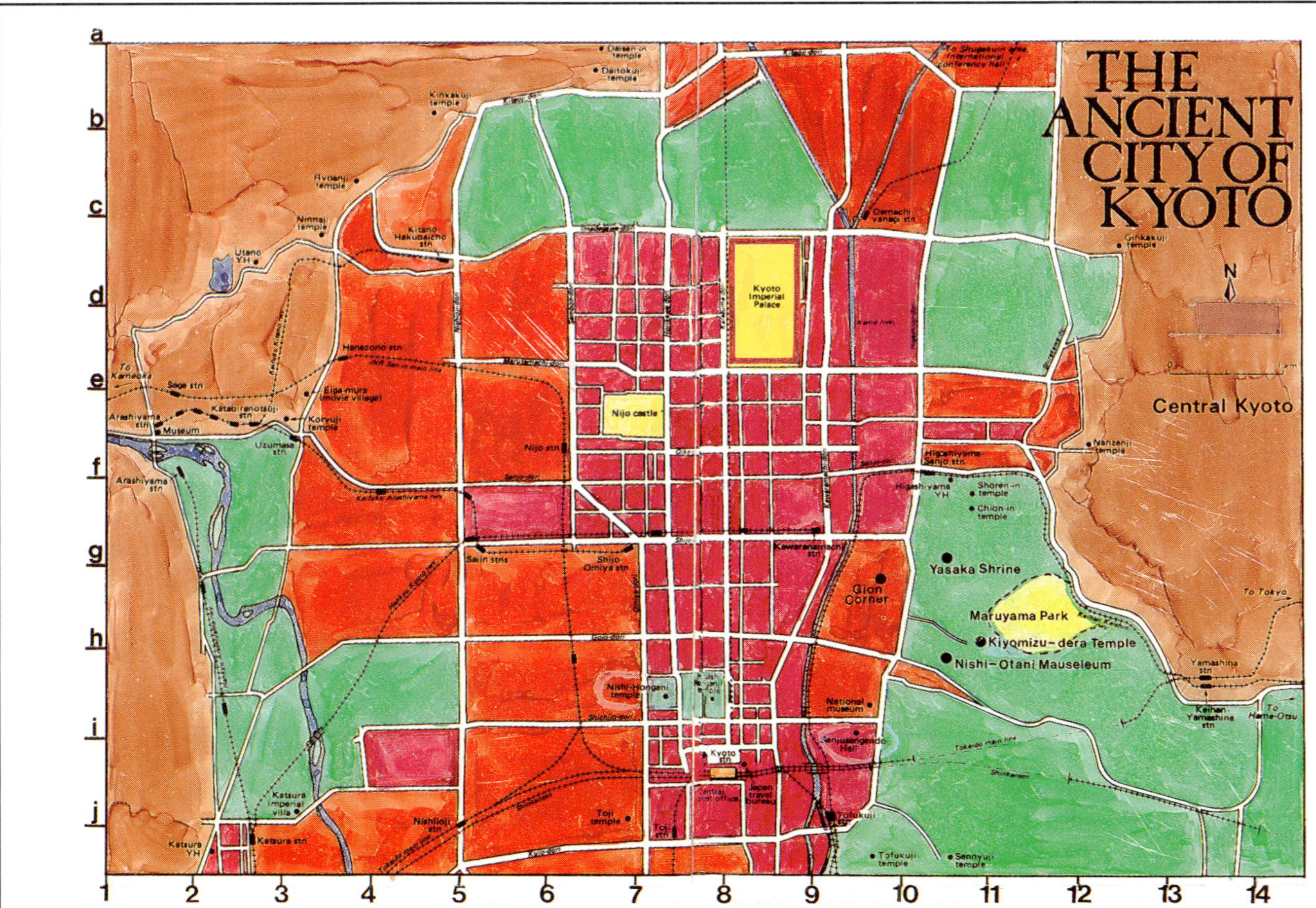

Kyoto, an inland city in central Japan, has been inhabited for over 1,000 years. In 794 A.D. Emperor Kanmu declared it the western capital of Japan. Kyoto had its golden age between the tenth and twelfth centuries. It was during this period that the culture of Japan flourished in the areas of architecture, arts, crafts and religious ceremonies. Until the Meiji Restoration in 1868, Kyoto had been the cultural and political center of Japan for almost 1,000 years.

route. "Let's stand right here," she said.

The parade had a lot of ceremony. Kenny explained that the people pulling the floats would exchange gifts as part of the festival. Every float was being pulled by "people power." It seemed as if everyone in *Nihon* was out to watch the parade. Across the street, workers leaned out the windows of their offices to watch the proceedings.

"The festival is such a family activity. It is especially nice to see the fathers spending time with their children. Look at that man and his son! The father is fanning the little boy!" I said.

"The tradition of doing things as a family unit and celebrating the traditions of the region have stood the test of time!" Kenny replied.

We decided to walk to the Imperial Palace. This was a large fenced area with a castle surrounded by a huge park.

"Kyoto seems to be a living museum or time capsule of the traditions and culture of *Nihon*," Mom said.

I went to bed that night with images of colorful floats, of fathers and sons dressed in *kimonos*, and of a delicious round watermelon! I could see the bright colors of the evening's fireworks reflected in the water outside the hotel. I drifted off to sleep with the sound of the fireworks exploding in the distance.

We got up early the next morning and got ready to go to ***Nara***. First we took the subway to the Tourist Information Center.

Floats are an important part of parades in Japan.

JAPAN REGIONS AND PREFECTURES

REGION Prefecture	CHIEF TOWN
HOKKAIDO	
1 Hokkaido	Sapporo
TOHOKU	
2 Aomori	Aomori
3 Akita	Akita
4 Iwate	Morioka
5 Yamagata	Yamagata
6 Miyagi	Sendai
7 Fukishima	Fukushima
KANTO	
8 Tochigi	Utsunomiya
9 Gumma	Maebashi
10 Ibaraki	Mito
11 Saitama	Urawa
12 Chiba	Chiba
13 Tokyo	Tokyo
14 Kanagawa	Yokohama
CHUBU	
15 Niigata	Niigata
16 Toyama	Toyama
17 Ishikawa	Kanazawa
18 Fukui	Fukui
19 Gifu	Gifu
20 Nagano	Nagano
21 Yamanshi	Kofu
22 Shizuoka	Shizuoka
23 Aichi	Nagoya
KANSAI	
24 Mie	Tsu
25 Shiga	Otsu
26 Kyoto	Kyoto
27 Hyogo	Kobe
28 Osaka	Osaka
29 Nara	Nara
30 Wakayama	Wakayama
31 Tottori	Tottori
32 Okayama	Okayama
33 Hiroshima	Hiroshima
34 Shimane	Matsue
35 Yamaguchi	Yamaguchi
SHIKOKU	
36 Kagawa	Takamatsu
37 Tokushima	Tokushima
38 Kochi	Kochi
39 Ehime	Matsuyama
KYUSHU	
40 Fukuoka	Fukuoka
41 Oita	Oita
42 Miyazaki	Miyazaki
43 Kumamoto	Kumamoto
44 Saga	Saga
45 Nagasaki	Nagasaki
46 Kagoshima	Kagoshima
47 Okinawa	Naha

Source: Government of Japan

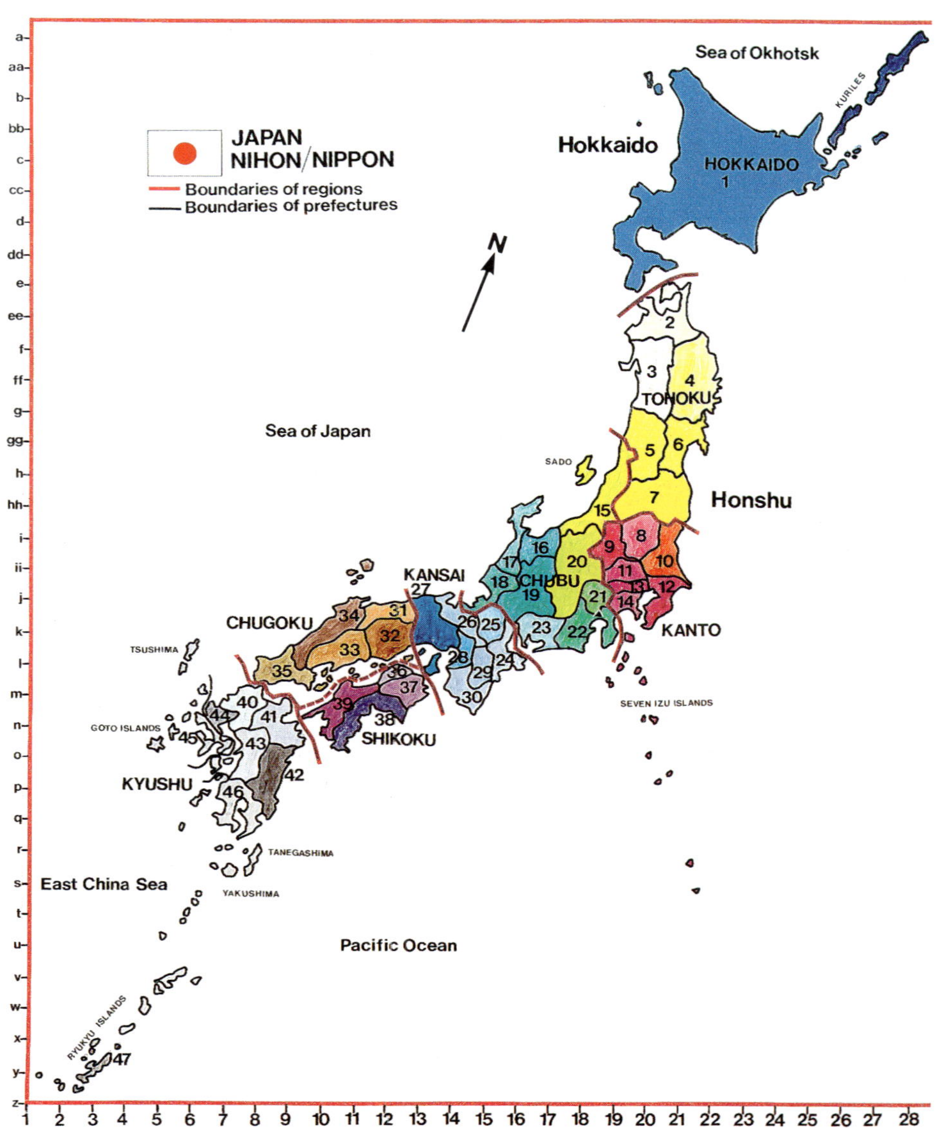

Japan's Government

Japan's Constitution was introduced on May 3, 1947. It transferred ruling power from the emperor to the people. The constitution guarantees rights and freedoms such as freedom of speech and religion and the right to vote. In Japan, all citizens have the right to vote at age twenty.

The Japanese parliament is called the Diet and is responsible for making laws. It is made up of two houses called the House of Representatives and the House of Councillors. Members of the House of Representatives are elected by election districts every four years. Some members of the House of Councillors are elected by the country as a whole while others are elected from districts called **prefectures**. Councillors serve a term of six years. The Diet building is located in Tokyo.

The prime minister of Japan is chosen by the Diet from among its members. The prime minister appoints the members of cabinet, half of whom must also be members of the Diet.

Japan is divided into forty-seven prefectures. Each prefecture has a governor and an assembly which is elected by voters in the prefecture. Within each prefecture there are cities, towns and villages with their own elected officials.

One modern convenience that Kyoto has accepted is a single line underground subway. We were glad, and our feet were too. A lady on the subway told Kenny that last week, during the typhoon, the subway was closed for two days because the heavy rains caused leaking and flooding in one section of the tunnel.

"I'm glad the typhoon is over. It is still the rainy season, and parts of the country are still being flooded," Kenny said.

We left the subway at the Tourist Information Center and a lady helped us find maps for our trip to Nara. She told us that *Nihon* has had different capitals and different forms of government throughout history. She went on to say that from 1192 to 1868, the country was ruled by the Shoguns. From 1868 until 1945 it had imperial rule and since 1947 *Nihon* has had a form of government similar to that of Canada and the U.S.

"Nara was the capital of *Nihon* from 710 to 794 A.D. Many of *Nihon's* cultural traditions, arts and crafts began in Nara," she said. "It is a very religious city. Millions of *Nihonjin* travel to Nara each year to pay a visit and honor deceased relatives whose shrines are in Nara. Nara is also the home of the famous ***Todai-ji Temple***," she informed us.

"That's where the statue of the Buddha Rushana is located. It is the world's largest bronze statue," Kenny added.

"We have to take the shuttle bus to Kyoto station and get on the JR commuter train," Dad said.

The commuter train was almost empty this morning. As we were leaving the city we could see another train coming towards us. It was so full that people were standing in the aisles. Another

Stone lanterns leading to the Kasuga Shrine.

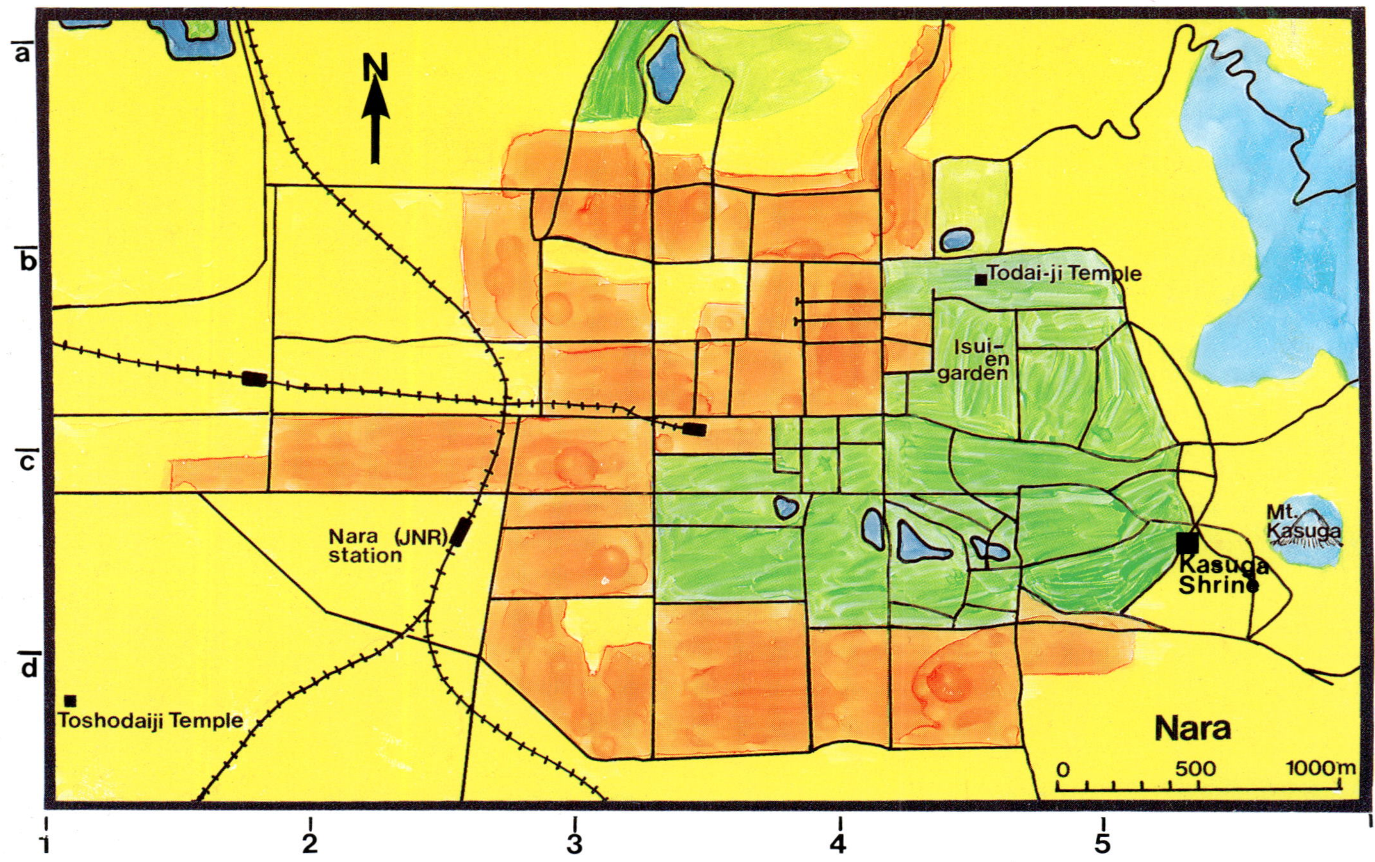

work day for the people of Kyoto! The trip to Nara lasted only about an hour.

"I sure am glad we are finally here. The train must have made at least fifteen to twenty stops!" I said.

"That is why they call it a commuter train. People who work in Kyoto live in each one of the towns we stopped at," Kenny replied.

When we arrived in Nara we spent about two and a half hours touring the ***Toshodoaiji Temple***. We were really impressed by everything we saw.

Then we visited the famous Todai-ji Temple. The size of the Buddha was amazing. I could not understand how such a huge statue could be made. We found out that it took three years just to cast and was completed in 749 A.D. Mom and Dad paid ¥1,000 for a roof tile. This donation would go towards the restoration of the temple. Mom used her calligraphy skills to paint our family name, address and date on the tile.

We went to the deer park and fed the deer. They were very tame. We sat and watched a man feeding ducks by the pond. It seemed as if the rest of the world did not exist. Finally Dad said it was time to go back to the train.

We made our way down paths lined by small shrines and returned to the JR station. We quickly grabbed some chicken and jumped on board the commuter train for our return trip to Kyoto. I had to laugh. The lady across the aisle from us had also picked up a fast-food chicken dinner for her family. So much for our visit to old *Nihon*.

(Above left) The deer at Nara park. (Above right) The great Buddha Rushana statue in front of the Todai-ji Temple is 15 meters high and weighs over 450,000 kilograms. (Above) The Todai-ji Temple at Nara.

Mom mentioned how good it was to see that the Japanese have continued to practice their spirit of worship. Nara is a city that easily accepts modern things, yet holds onto the important religious traditions.

I will always remember Kenny saying: "Japanese children grow up thinking that McDonald's is part of the Japanese culture but they also learn the importance of art, nature and respect for all things."

I thought of homes with plants and trees. Images of moms, dads, uncles and aunts looking after and playing with the children passed through my mind. Along with these images were glimpses of people rushing to be on time for work yet taking the time to smell the flowers. I also wondered about the contrasts between: shrines and electronic inventions, wooden and concrete buildings.

My ability to understand and speak in the language was getting better. I was even beginning to dream in *Nihongo*. Each day I wanted to know more and more about this country. I reminded myself to ask Kenny a simple but important question: How is rice grown? I thought I knew but I wanted to be sure.

More of the past would arrive tomorrow. . . .

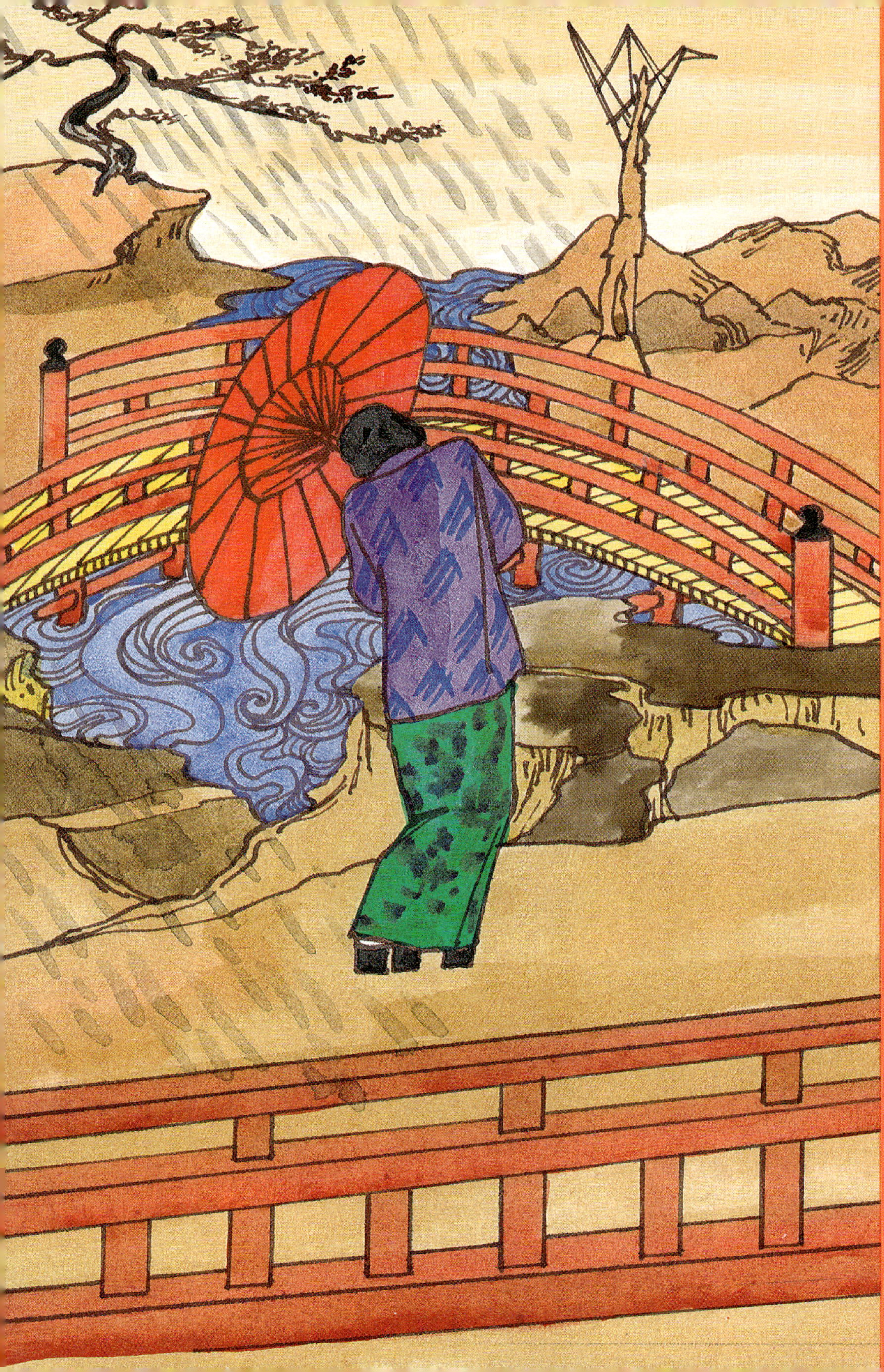

Chapter 8

MAY WE NEVER FORGET THE HORROR

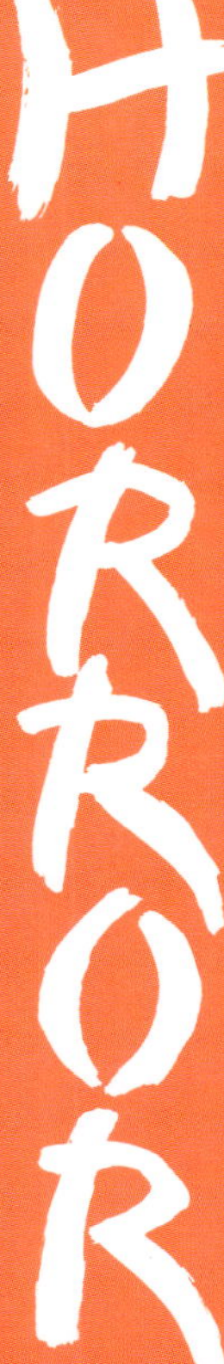

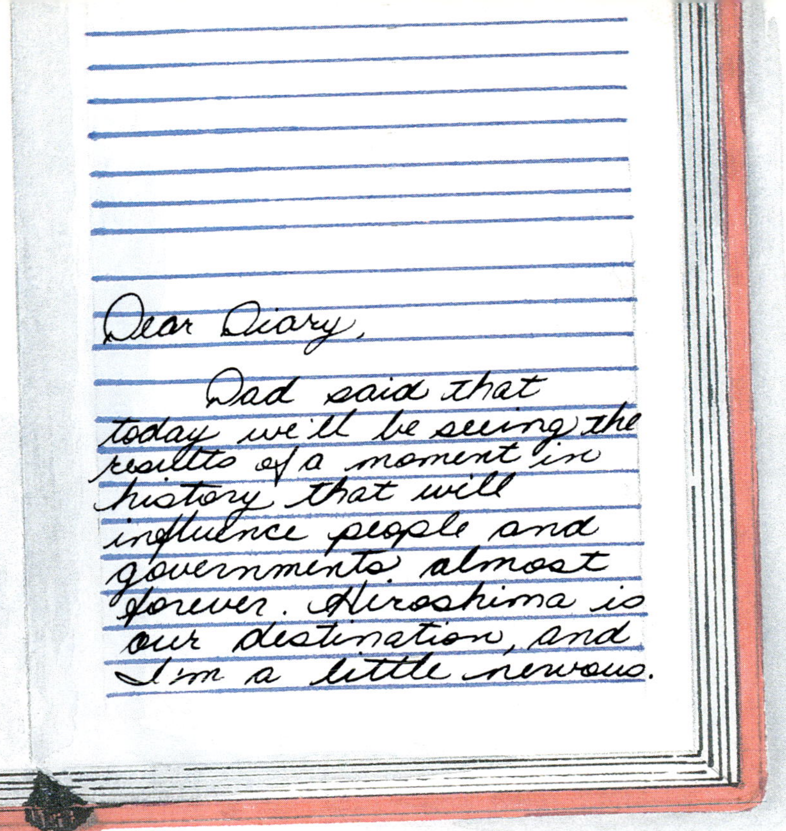

We took the bus to **_Gion Corner_** in Kyoto because it was really raining. We decided to go and see the Yasaka Shrine and Maruyama Park. Both were beautiful and peaceful – even in the rain. It seemed like we walked for miles and miles. We eventually ended up at Gojozaka. We thought we had only gone to the Yasaka Pagoda. "We are at the Nishi-Otani Mausoleum," Kenny said. "This is a famous burial site. There are hundreds of monuments and small shrines on the grounds."

We then went back towards Sannenzaka. "I could spend days looking in all of the little open air shops!" I exclaimed.

"We'll meet you at the Kiyomizu and Jojuin Temples," Dad replied.

I continued to shop and visit with the people in the stores. Everyone was so polite and friendly. Japanese girls kept asking me if they could speak with me and practice their English. I felt really important.

I walked up the narrow path to the temples and

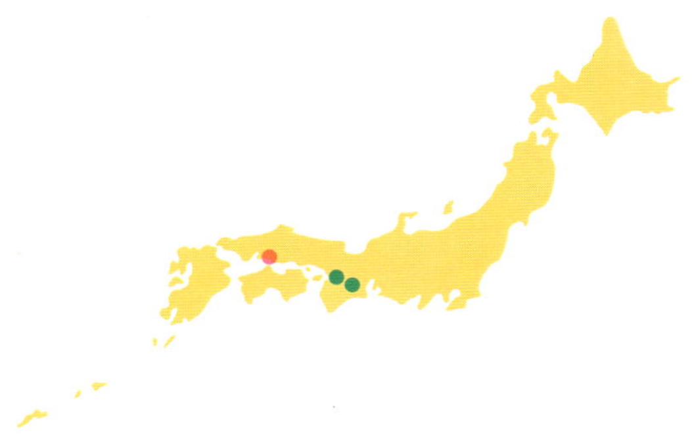

met Mom. She pointed to the other side of the hill and I could see Kenny and Dad waving back to us. They seemed to be in another world. Everything had a dream-like quality to it. I imagined nobles and *samurai* walking along the paths. I could see the *geisha* performing their ceremonies in the tea house. I imagined the pilgrims standing at the entrance to the temple. When we walked back down the narrow path we passed hundreds of people going up to the temples. It was still raining

Pilgrim in front of temple.

very hard. Therefore, we decided to get back on bus No. 206. After about twenty minutes Kenny said that the bus went all around the city. Mom just shrugged her shoulders and said, "We might as well enjoy the scenic tour of Kyoto. At least we are out of the rain."

We had noodles and fish for supper in a small and quiet restaurant. As we returned to our hotel a crowd of people were unloading from a tour bus. I said to Kenny, "I'm glad we are travelling by ourselves and are not part of a tour." He laughed and replied,"Yeah! How else would you have enough time to shop?"

The next day we went to Hiroshima.

We left our hotel at 10:00 A.M. While waiting for the Shinkensen, Kenny and I bought *bento*s for all of us. When our train left the *eki* Kenny pointed to the digital speedometer and said: "Look we are travelling at 214 kilometers per hour. Our trip will only take about two hours going through Osaka."

When we arrived in Hiroshima Dad suggested that we just walk around and get the feel for the place.

"Tomorrow you will see some of the most shocking things you have seen in your life," Dad said. "The events of World War II changed the lives of the Japanese and Americans forever."

I was almost scared by the way Dad said this. I asked Kenny if he knew what Dad meant. Kenny whispered that tomorrow would be soon enough. I fell asleep wondering what lessons of the past I was about to learn.

We started our discovery of Hiroshima very early in the morning. We visited a Japanese Garden called Shukkei-en Garden. I said to Mom: "It is so quiet and peaceful. We must have beaten the crowds. We are the only ones here in the park."

"Well, almost the only people," Mom replied. "Kenny seems to have found a new friend."

I walked over to a bench where Kenny was sitting and talking to an older man. Kenny said: "Lorraine, this is Mr. Ito from Los Angeles. His granddaughter is a famous figure skater from Sapporo."

"Konnichi-wa Ito-san," I said.

"*Ohayo gozaimasu*, Lorraine," replied Mr. Ito. "This is a beautiful garden. I came early to avoid the crowds. I was here yesterday but all of the people kept disturbing my thoughts. I'm glad I came back here today."

"We will leave you alone if you like," I offered.

"Thank you but that is not necessary. I greeted the morning and watched the sun rise. Have you thought about how, for the Eastern World, the sun rises over *Nihon* to begin each day? That is why Japan is known as 'The Land of the Rising Sun'."

"Mr. Ito, did you live in *Nihon* before moving to Los Angeles?" asked Kenny.

"Yes, I lived in the prefecture of Tottori-ken when I was a little boy," he replied.

"Tottori-ken! That's where Kenny's grandparents are from," I exclaimed.

Mr. Ito smiled and continued, "I remember the land as being one of the prettiest places on earth."

I asked Mr. Ito if he had been in the war. A sad look came over his face. "My father moved my mother, my sister and me before there were even problems between *Nihon* and the rest of the world," he began. "We lived in Vancouver, British Columbia and then Los Angeles, California. My grandfather was in the Japanese navy during World War II. I was very young. I did not understand why my *ojiisan* was an enemy to my new home. I did not understand why we were treated so badly by our new neighbors. I guess everybody was scared."

"Would you tell me a little bit about the war and Hiroshima? I know that something awful happened here but I really don't understand it. Can you help me to understand?" I asked.

"I don't know if anyone can really explain the reasons and the horror of war, Lorraine. I can tell

"All the News That's Fit to Print."

The New York Times.

LATE CITY EDITION
Increasing cloudiness with rising temperature today. Tomorrow cloudy, somewhat colder.
Temperatures Yesterday—Max.,34; Min.,25

Copyright, 1941, by The New York Times Company.

VOL. XCI No. 30,634. Entered as Second-Class Matter, Postoffice, New York, N. Y. NEW YORK, MONDAY, DECEMBER 8, 1941. THREE CENTS NEW YORK CITY and Vicinity

JAPAN WARS ON U. S. AND BRITAIN; MAKES SUDDEN ATTACK ON HAWAII; HEAVY FIGHTING AT SEA REPORTED

CONGRESS DECIDED

Roosevelt Will Address It Today and Find It Ready to Vote War

CONFERENCE IS HELD

Legislative Leaders and Cabinet in Sober White House Talk

By C. P. TRUSSELL
Special to THE NEW YORK TIMES.

WASHINGTON, Dec. 7—President Roosevelt will address a joint session of Congress tomorrow and will find the membership in a mood to vote any steps he asks in connection with the developments in the Pacific.

The President will appear personally at 12:30 P. M. Whether he would call for a flat declaration of war again Japan was left unannounced tonight. But leaders of Congress, shocked and angered by the Japanese attacks, were talking of a declaration of war on not only Japan but on the entire Axis.

The plans for action tomorrow were made tonight in a White House conference at which the President, surrounded by his Cabinet and by Congressional leaders of both parties, went through reports, some official, some unconfirmed, of the continued assaults of the Japanese upon American Pacific outposts.

Meet Far Into Night

The conference lasted until after

TOKYO ACTS FIRST

Declaration Follows Air and Sea Attacks on U. S. and Britain

TOGO CALLS ENVOYS

After Fighting Is On, Grew Gets Japan's Reply to Hull Note of Nov. 26

By The Associated Press.

TOKYO, Monday, Dec. 8—Japan went to war against the United States and Britain today with air and sea attacks against Hawaii, followed by a formal declaration of hostilities.

Japanese Imperial headquarters announced at 6 A. M. [4 P. M. Sunday, Eastern standard time] that a state of war existed among these nations in the Western Pacific, as of dawn.

Soon afterward, Domei, the Japanese official news agency, announced that "naval operations are progressing off Hawaii, with at least one Japanese aircraft carrier in action against Pearl Harbor," the American naval base in the islands.

Japanese bombers were declared to have raided Honolulu at 7:35 A. M., Hawaii time [1:05 Sunday, Eastern standard time].

Premier-War Minister General Hideki Tojo held a twenty-minute Cabinet session at his official residence at 7 A. M.

Soon afterward it was announced

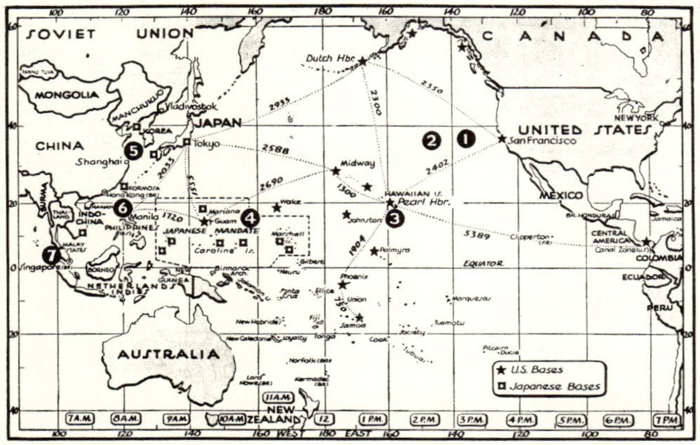

PACIFIC OCEAN: THEATRE OF WAR INVOLVING UNITED STATES AND ITS ALLIES

Shortly after the outbreak of hostilities an American ship sent a distress call from (1) and a United States Army transport carrying lumber was torpedoed at (2). The most important action was at Hawaii (3), where Japanese planes bombed the great Pearl Harbor base. Also attacked was Guam (4). From Manila (6) United States bombers roared northward, while some parts of the Philippines were raided, as was Hong Kong, to the northwest. At Shanghai (5) a British gunboat was sunk and an American gunboat seized. To the south, in the Malaya area (7), the British bombed Japanese ships, Tokyo forces attempted landings on British territory and Singapore underwent an air raid. Distances between key Pacific points are shown on the map in statute miles.

JAPANESE FORCE LANDS IN MALAYA

First Attempt Is Repulsed—Singapore Is Bombed and Thailand Invaded

Tokyo Bombers Strike Hard At Our Main Bases on Oahu

By The United Press.

HONOLULU, Dec. 7—War broke with lightning suddenness in the Pacific today when waves of Japanese bombers attacked Hawaii this morning and the United States Fleet struck back with a thunder of big naval rifles. Japanese bombers, including four

HULL DENOUNCES TOKYO 'INFAMY'

Brands Japan 'Fraudulent' in Preparing Attack While Carrying On Parleys

GUAM BOMBED; ARMY SHIP IS SUNK

U. S. Fliers Head North From Manila—Battleship Oklahoma Set Afire by Torpedo Planes at Honolulu

104 SOLDIERS KILLED AT FIELD IN HAWAII

President Fears 'Very Heavy Losses' on Oahu—Churchill Notifies Japan That a State of War Exists

By FRANK L. KLUCKHOHN
Special to THE NEW YORK TIMES.

WASHINGTON, Monday, Dec. 8—Sudden and unexpected attacks on Pearl Harbor, Honolulu, and other United States possessions in the Pacific early yesterday by the Japanese air force and navy plunged the United States and Japan into active war.

The initial attack in Hawaii, apparently launched by torpedo-carrying bombers and submarines, caused widespread damage and death. It was quickly followed by others. There were unconfirmed reports that German raiders participated in the attacks.

Guam also was assaulted from the air, as were Davao, on the island of Mindanao, and Camp John Hay, in Northern Luzon, both in the Philippines. Lieut. Gen. Douglas MacArthur, commanding the United States Army of the Far East, reported there was little damage, however.

[Japanese parachute troops had been landed in the Philippines and native Japanese had seized some communities, Royal Arch Gunnison said in a broadcast from Manila today to WOR-Mutual. He reported without detail that "in the naval war the ABCD fleets under American command appeared to be successful" against Japanese invasions.]

Japanese submarines, ranging out over the Pacific, sank an American transport carrying lumber 1,300 miles from San Francisco, and distress signals were heard from a freighter 700 miles from that city.

you a few details. The rest you will see for yourself later today. What you must remember is that people have always acted in ways that have hurt others. The Second World War hurt so much that the people of Hiroshima are dedicated to worldwide peace. Some want to make sure that no one ever forgets how the tragedy happened. Others who lived through the war are still trying to forget and get on with their lives."

"Mr. Ito, you said that Hiroshima was something that the people wanted to remember and forget. Why would they want it to be both ways?" I asked.

"Lorraine, I am afraid that you will only understand that after you have seen both sides of Hiroshima – the old and the new. The new is like this peaceful park. The old will show you the great horrors of war. Japan is a country that was greatly changed by World War II. All of the country's efforts have been channeled into production and the maintenance of peace," responded Mr. Ito. "Now let's just sit here and listen to the birds and watch the sun travel across the water," he said.

We left Mr. Ito and went to Hiroshima Castle. It was five stories tall. The lady at the desk gave us a present of postcards. Inside the castle the original armor of the *samurai* warriors was on display. From the top of the castle we could see many old

JAPAN IN THE SECOND WORLD WAR

In September of 1940 Japan was advancing into Northern Indochina in an effort to obtain more territory and resources for its growing population. In order to restrict this expansion, the United States imposed an oil embargo on Japan in 1941.

The Japanese leaders devised a strategy to defeat the United States navy and air force and thus be free of the trade restrictions. At 8 A.M. on Sunday, December 7, 1941, Japanese carrier-based planes bombed Pearl Harbor in the Hawaiian Islands. The results included severe human and military losses. The United States declared war with Japan on December 8, 1941. Many battles were fought in the islands of the Pacific Ocean over the next three years.

The regular bombing of Japan began in November 1944. The fighting continued into the summer of 1945. Both sides had suffered many losses. The Japanese used Kamikaze pilots who attacked enemy ships by crashing their planes into them.These men considered the act of suicide to be an honor in the tradition of the Samurai warriors.

While the fighting was going on, the United States government was secretly building a new weapon – an atomic bomb. They tested the first bomb in Alamogordo, New Mexico on July 16, 1945. They built two additional bombs to the one tested. President Harry S Truman allowed these two bombs to be dropped on Japan in order to save American lives. Several targets were picked as possible drop sites. One bomb was dropped on Hiroshima on August 6, 1945 and a second bomb was dropped on Nagasaki on August 9, 1945. The United States estimates that the number who died in Hiroshima was 66,000 to 78,000 and in Nagasaki there were 39,000. Japanese estimates give a combined total of 240,000 people.

On August 14, 1945, Japan announced its surrender. The formal signing of the agreement took place on September 2, 1945 in Tokyo Bay aboard the battleship Missouri.

The Japanese surrendered aboard the U.S.S. Missouri on September 2, 1945.

stone squares in the ground, where other walls of the castle had once stood. I heard Dad say to Mom: "It is hard to believe that they have completely rebuilt this castle."

Before lunch we also visited the Hiroshima Art Museum. "This is one of the finest collections of European artists in the world!" Mom said. She was obviously impressed!

We started the afternoon in the Peace Memorial Park. "You can see how powerful the atomic bomb must have been," Dad said. "This building shell is all that is left of the original city." I felt sad, quiet, sick and shocked all at once. I wondered why this had happened.

As we walked along I asked Mom, "How did anyone rebuild Hiroshima after suffering through the shock of the bomb? How did the people survive and go on? Why didn't they just give up and quit?"

"They were a proud and noble people," she said. "Remember that they always rebuilt after natural disasters. This was one more very big disaster."

Kenny added: "It is easy to see why the war ended. I can't imagine anyone who has seen this starting a nuclear war."

"Out of the mouth of babes!" Dad said. Kenny and I didn't understand what he meant.

Mom simply said: "You're very right, Kenny."

We toured through the War Memorial. The pictures were very realistic. They made you feel like you were there, and they made you want to run away. We saw photos, burnt clothing, maps, and pieces of concrete where shadows had been burned into them forever. We read of the help given to the survivors. We also learned that people suffered for many years after the initial bombing from radiation-related diseases. I didn't know what atomic burns were or what radiation was but I could sense the pain and I could see the agony. "I have to go outside. I need some air. I think I'm going to be sick!" I said.

The War Memorial Park in Hiroshima.

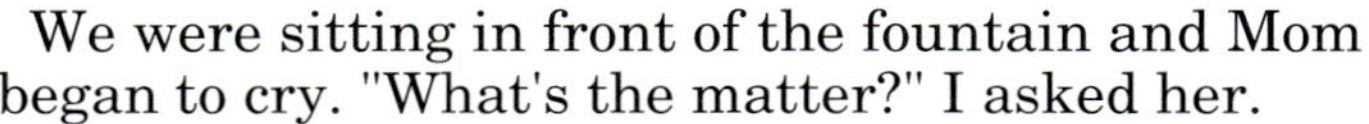

We were sitting in front of the fountain and Mom began to cry. "What's the matter?" I asked her.

She wiped away the tears and she said, "I just feel sad." Dad suggested a walk in the park to take us away from what we had just seen and heard. We all agreed.

In the park three girls came up to Kenny and me and asked if they could practice speaking English with us. Kenny puffed out his chest and said: "Why, of course. What would you like to talk about?"

The girls giggled and whispered to themselves. Finally one of them said: "Thank you, but no, we would like to speak with you." She was pointing at me.

We introduced ourselves.

The one called Tamiko asked: "Where are you from? What do you think of Hiroshima? What do you think of World Peace?"

"I am from a town called Beaver Creek in California," I answered. "Kenny is from Tokyo. We believe that everyone should work towards world peace. Hiroshima is a lovely city. The people are very friendly. There are many shocking memories of the bombing though."

Tamiko said: "This statue was built and paid for by young people throughout Japan who wanted to honor Sadako Sasaki and other children who were killed by the bomb or died afterwards from leukemia."

"Your parents must have horrible memories of the war," I said to her.

SADAKO SASAKI

Sadako Sasaki was two years old when the atomic bomb was dropped on Hiroshima. She appeared healthy until the age of ten, when it was discovered that she had leukemia caused by radiation.

While Sadako was in the hospital, a friend brought her a crane made of gold paper. Sadako was reminded of the legend of the crane. The crane is supposed to live for one thousand years, and if Sadako folded one thousand paper cranes, the gods would make her healthy again and she would not die. Sadako spent her time making cranes, bravely facing her pain and illness.

When she died on October 25, 1955, she had folded 644 paper cranes. Her classmates folded the remaining 356 so that one thousand could be buried with her.

In 1958, the Children's Peace Monument was built in her memory. On Peace Day, August 6 of each year, young people place paper cranes beneath her statue.

Paper cranes are placed at the Children's Peace Monument.

"Yes," she answered quietly, "my mother still bears her burn scars of the bombing. She reminds me that we must work hard to keep the world at peace. We want to be productive and yet work with others. I would like to be your friend," she said.

I told them all that I would like to be their friend. Kenny added,"Me too!" We all laughed and exchanged some small pins. They gave us little paper dolls and paper birds of peace. We exchanged names and addresses and promised to write to one another.

We left the park and walked a long way to Hijiyama Park. "This uphill walk is too long!" I complained without success. Dad wanted to see the city from above. From that viewpoint it was possible to see the ocean harbor. Also below us was a huge burial area. I thought again of the number of dead after the bombing.

"The Japanese have suffered through a lot to be successful today," Dad said. "All of the countries involved in the wars must share in the blame. Many of the Japanese strongly blame their own leaders for the horrors of Hiroshima. Most people never want Japan to be a military power again. The army is only for defense. One of the reasons for the success of the people is their ability to carry on. They have dedicated themselves to making a better life. They have built beauty and productivity where ruins and ashes existed less than fifty years ago."

"Japan and its people are beautiful," Mom added. "But today was necessary for you to understand that the beliefs, traditions and customs of the people, their acceptance of diversity and of opposites, and their living for today with a belief in an afterlife are all a part of having survived great tragedies."

"The Japanese have always rebuilt after fires, earthquakes, floods and the bombings. It is an accepted way of living," Kenny said.

Supper was stir fried vegetables, strips of beef, and rice. The small restaurant was cheery and bright. It was a good way to end the day. There was a calm and determined spirit about the Japanese that I could not explain. I did not know if anyone back home would ever understand this when I tried to tell them. There were so many contradictions. Cities could be so clean and yet so dirty in many ways. People could be overly polite and yet pushy. There was beauty and urban sprawl side by side. What road would we travel tomorrow?

This was the only building that survived the bomb.

Kenny said that the Japanese are trained from the time they are very young to move the body to a place of beauty, happiness and peace by using the mind. He said that it is possible to shut out the ugliness of the everyday world by thinking in a quiet garden. It must be true. Just thinking about Hiyijama Park helped me to get over the shocking things we had seen.

"You must try to see the positive side of the bombing of Hiroshima, Lorraine," Dad said. "I know it's hard to think about but consider this: The war did end very quickly. Japan concentrated its efforts on rebuilding a nation without a military except for defense. All of the people's efforts and money could go into rebuilding their lives and homes. Other countries throughout the world helped to develop schools, industry and trade. Medical scientists joined forces to treat the victims. The horrors of the bombing made everyone stop and think about what a destructive power nuclear war really was."

"But Ted, you must admit it is hard to think of the positive so soon after seeing the destruction!" argued Mom.

"I am not saying that we should ever forget the bombing of Hiroshima," continued Dad. "All I

Most of Hiroshima has been rebuilt.

meant was that Lorraine needs to think about the things that the Japanese are and have today that exist because of the war. The efforts to rebuild and become a powerful non-military nation were successful because of the total destruction!"

"My dad believes that the Japanese people never wanted to be in a war again after Hiroshima," Kenny said. "They then put all of their effort into keeping the good things in life. They put Hiroshima in a back corner of their mind. They got on with trying to prove to the world that they were a good and civilized people. They wanted to get on with their lives."

"I feel like I've grown up a lot on this trip, Mom," I said. "Japan is a beautiful and interesting place but it is also very complicated."

"Let's enjoy Miyajima and then talk more about it tomorrow," said Mom.

We took the train and the ferry to the island of Miyajima. The first thing we saw as we got nearer to the island was a huge red shrine sticking out of the water. We toured the temple and then went to the aquarium. "Let's go see the sea lion show!" I shouted.

"Look at the little children all dressed in the same uniforms," said Kenny. "They are part of a kindergarten school class."

We went on to watch the feeding of the fish and then to a huge tank that was home to a bunch of sea otters. Like many of the adult Japanese, Mom had her nose pressed to the window and was watching every move.

We then went to a viewpoint at the top of a mountain. The trees were very tall and thick below us. It was like we were going to the top of the world! We could see islands and ships out in the ocean. At the top of the hill, we found a monkey park. We also bought some souvenir rice paddles, and then made our way back to the ferry. "The soldiers from America sent these paddles home as souvenirs when they were serving here in Japan after the war," said Dad.

I immediately began to think again about the bombing of Hiroshima. Mom must have known by my face because she immediately said, "Ted, let's wait a few days before we talk more about the war."

The Miyajima gateway and shrine.

"It's okay Mrs. Kuilboer," said Kenny. "We talk about the tragedy and benefits of the war all the time at home."

"Well, I still think we should give Lorraine more time to think about it on her own before we discuss it further," argued Mom.

"Thanks, Mom," was all I could say. Then I began to cry. I just couldn't help it.

Chapter 9

THE FUTURE COMES QUICKLY

JAPANESE VOCABULARY

WORDS

dojo	doh•joh	judo hall
judo	ju•doh	martial arts

PHRASES and SENTENCES

Arigato Gozaimasu	Are•ee•gat•oh goh•zai•mah•sue	Thank you
Moshi, moshi!	moosh•ee moosh•ee	Hello (on the telephone)

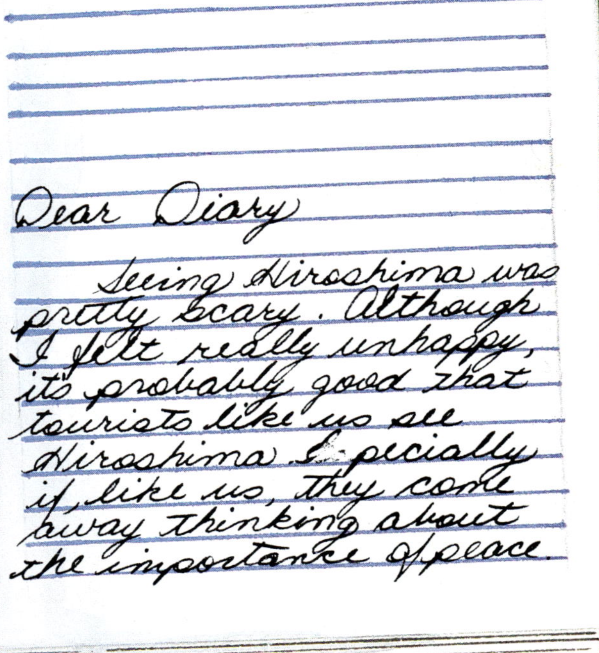

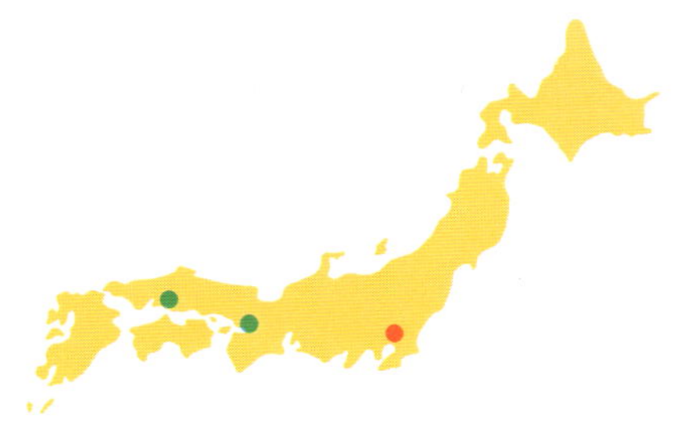

We got on board the Shinkansen Express and zoomed along towards Osaka. Kenny wondered if he would get a glimpse of one of *Nihon*'s most famous landmarks, Mt. Fuji.

A man at the train station, who spoke very good *Eigo*, gave us directions to our hotel. We quickly checked in and had lunch at a restaurant. There was a grill in the center of our table. "We will be able to cook our own meal," Kenny said. "You choose fish, meats and vegetables from the menu and then cook them on the grill."

It was a very good meal. As we were leaving, the owner of the restaurant said: "You use *hashi* very well," and he gave me some *hashi* wrapped in colored paper.

"ARIGATO GOZAIMASU," (*are•ee•gat•oh goh•zai•mah•sue* - thank you) I said.

Returning to the big city reminded us of how hot it was in *Nihon* during the summer. We heard that Tokyo had a major power failure one day because everyone was using their air conditioners. Ten percent of 13,000 traffic lights

ENERGY NEEDS

Japan's huge industries, its transportation system and cities have created a never-ending thirst for fuel and electrical power. Thermo-electricity generated by burning oil is now being supplemented by atomic energy. In addition, Japan also has numerous oil refineries that process imported oil. Most of these plants are found along the Pacific coast.

Ginza district in Tokyo.

The INTEX Center. Inset: The newly developed curve escalator.

went out, and elevators and subways stopped running. Fortunately quick thinking and action by power crews and police kept traffic and people moving. The power was quickly restored by using the power from a brand new thermal power plant.

We figured out the subway routes and went to the port area of the city. We saw lots of container ships, lumber yards, logs in the bay, and high rise complexes.

"There are forty-eight buildings all alike and they are twelve to fifteen stories high. Housing is so high in price that people wait many years to move into one of these complexes," Kenny said.

At the International Exhibition Center (INTEX) in Osaka we learned that Japanese companies were, in fact, trading all over the world. Many of these companies own large companies in North America. We learned that *Nihon* is the world's largest importer of lumber. We also had a man tell us about Japan's Space Program. The *Nihonjin* are making rapid advancements in the telecommunications field and are developing their own satellite launching program. We were told about a company called Nissho Iwai. A tape from the videotape library of INTEX explained that Nissho Iwai's head office is in Osaka. The company also has major offices in Tokyo, New York and London. Nissho Iwai is involved in imports, exports, communications, and domestic production. The company is also an agent for Boeing aircraft. They even provided steel pipe and a floating deck to the Trans Alaska Pipeline project. And, they are involved in offshore oil drilling projects. They are also producing liquid natural gas in Indonesia. Companies such as this are helping *Nihon* to trade with the world.

After we left INTEX we went back downtown to the street mall area. That was all right with me.

"It sure is hot out today!" I complained.

"Let's just step inside this air-conditioned shopping mall to cool off," said Kenny.

"Good idea," said Dad. "It sure is hard to get around this city without being able to read *Kanji*. Kenny, you will have to help me with directions."

"No problem," Kenny replied.

"Mom, have you noticed that people continue to look at us? I really feel that we stand out from the crowd," I said.

"Well, Lorraine, you must admit we do look different than the thousands of *Nihonjin* that surround us," replied Mom.

"Sometimes I like the attention and then sometimes I just want to be one of the crowd," I continued.

"We are doing quite well at fitting in and getting around. People have been good to us!" said Mom.

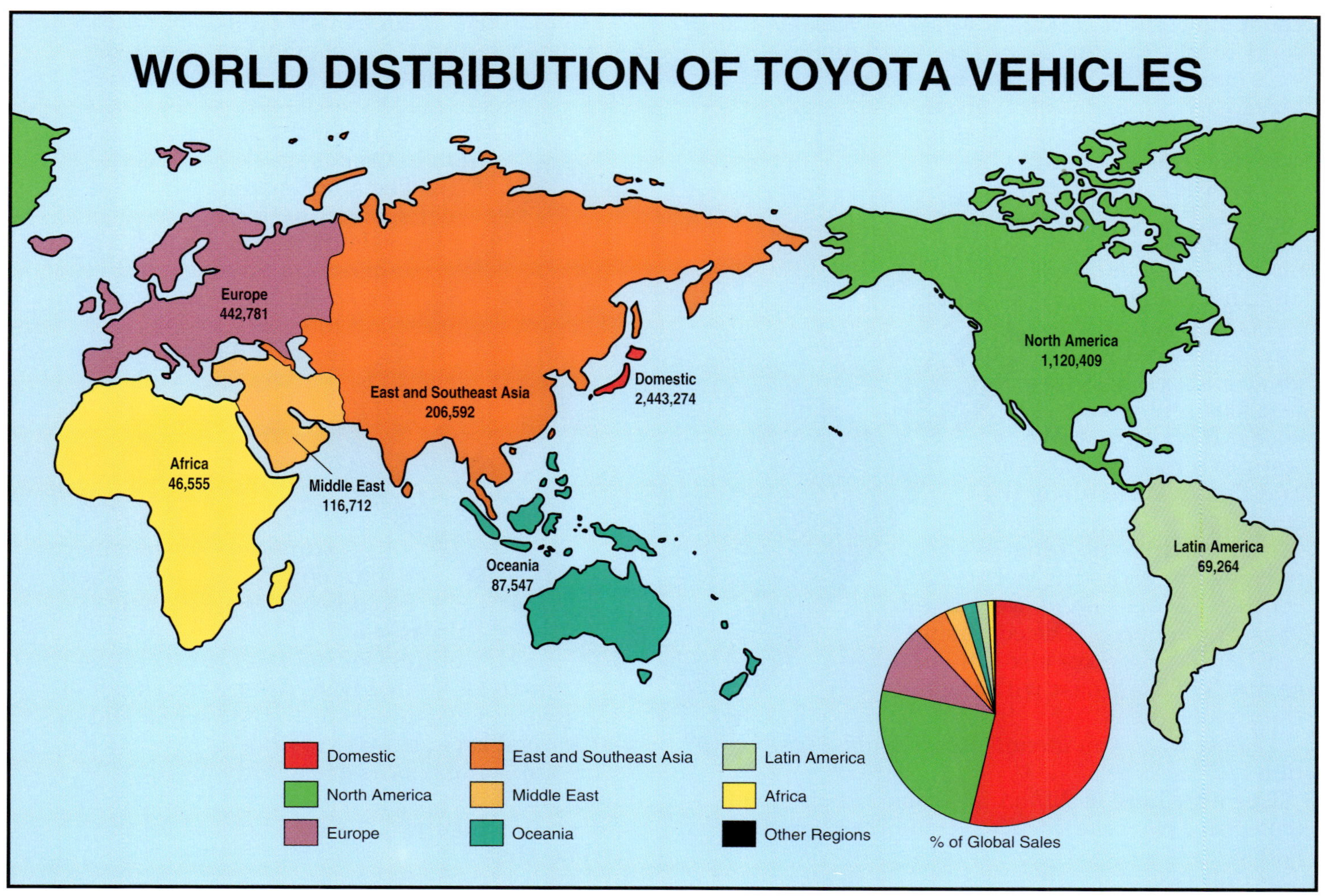

Back at the hotel we watched a huge fireworks festival on television. After the show on the news they said that a lottery for condominium units had 3,000 people apply for one hundred units.

Dad phoned Mr. Adachi to confirm our arrival in Tokyo. I had to laugh at his pronunciation of the telephone word in Japanese for hello. He said, "*MOSHI, MOSHI* (moosh•ee moosh•ee-hello)."

"Like mooshi mooshi?" I kidded. "It sounds like a sick cow!"

We went back out to do a little shopping. The Japanese have a maze of very good underground shopping centers. I bought a jacket for ¥500 and some bright wooden shoes that were made by a man who put the shoe and straps together right in the store. Kenny came up behind me: "Look at this neat poster I bought. It is from the Tenjin Matsuri Festival."

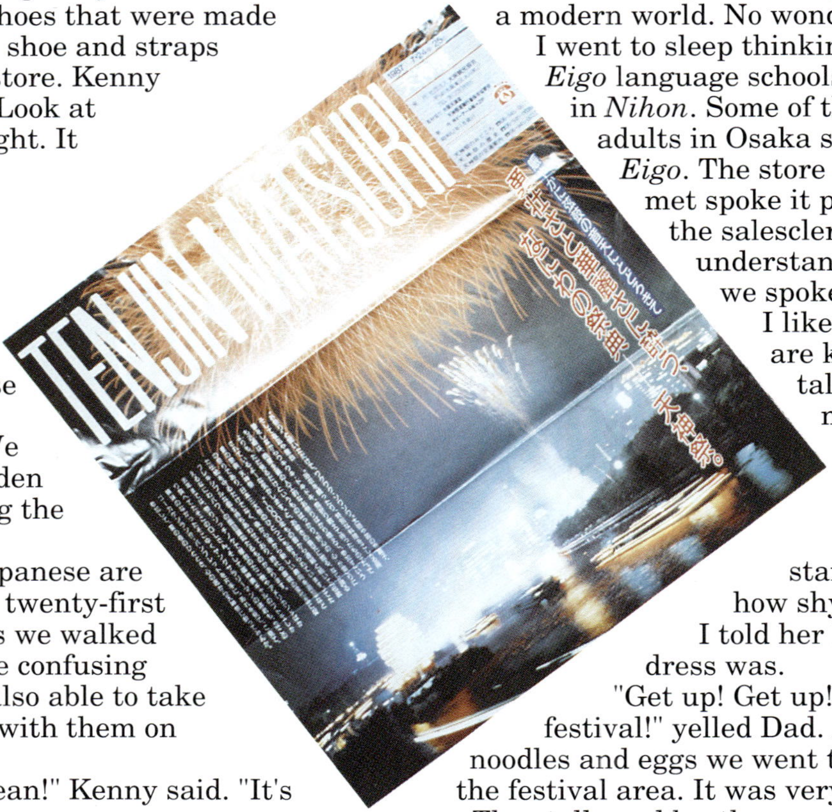

Mom found another *kimono* and Dad bought a wood block print. We found one area where you could get Japanese fast food and baked goods. It was great. We went to a roof top garden and then walked along the canal.

"It seems like the Japanese are in a rush to get to the twenty-first century," Mom said as we walked back to the hotel. "The confusing part is that they are also able to take so much of their past with them on their journey."

"I know what you mean!" Kenny said. "It's like . . ."

"Life over here in *Nihon* is a constant choice of travelling two roads: the past and the present," I added.

When we walked back into the hotel room Dad and Kenny were talking about a news story involving the Toshiba company. Dad was trying to explain to Kenny that the United States was upset that the company had traded military parts to Russia.

"The president of the company will probably resign over this," Kenny said.

"Why would he resign over something as small as that?" I asked.

"It is a matter of saving face and national honor," Kenny replied. "His resignation is a way of saying he is sorry. It is a big deal."

There it was again. A very traditional act in a modern world. No wonder I'm confused.

I went to sleep thinking about how the *Eigo* language schools are so important in *Nihon*. Some of the students and adults in Osaka speak very good *Eigo*. The store manager that we met spoke it perfectly. However, the salesclerk could not understand anything until we spoke *Nihongo*.

I like the fact that kids are kids. It is easy to talk to boys and girls my own age. I had fun with the girls in McDonald's who told me about their favorite music stars. I also remember how shy Tamiko was when I told her how pretty her dress was.

"Get up! Get up! It's the day of the festival!" yelled Dad. After a breakfast of noodles and eggs we went to the temple and the festival area. It was very hot!

The stalls and booths are mainly for little children.

"It's like a carnival," I said. "Look at all the food booths."

Osaka Castle has been rebuilt many times.

Later we went across the river and had a short rest. We then decided to tour Osaka Castle. The castle has been rebuilt and is modernized with an elevator up but stairs down. The castle was impressive with grounds that were large and well maintained. The art work or silkscreens told the story of the feudal wars.

"These battles look very much like the stories you read to me about early England. It looks like the kings and their knights," I said.

"You have a good point, Lorraine. This part of early Japanese history was very much like that of early England," said Dad approvingly. So far apart and yet so similar, I thought. I wonder why?

As we walked along the grounds Kenny said: "There's a *DOJO* (*doh•joh*-judo hall). It's a hall being used for *JUDO* (*ju•doh*-martial art) lessons." The *Sensei* still command great respect from the students.

"Look, there are a few girls in the class," I whispered to Mom. A man standing next to me said: "Girls are allowed in the sessions. There are often four hundred students in these sessions. The sessions run all day, every day. Students take *judo* and other martial arts as part of the Physical Education program in Senior High School."

We sat on a small wall in the garden and watched the sun begin to set. We decided it was time to go and watch the boat parade. As we moved towards the river, Mom said: "Lorraine, you and Kenny stay right in front of Dad and me! I've never seen so many people in one place. We don't want to get separated."

"Don't worry. We aren't going anywhere," I answered.

I had never seen this many people in one place either. It was like we were moving with the flow of the river. We crossed the bridge and then found a quiet spot near the bank where we could watch the parade. The quiet lasted for two minutes.

All of a sudden the spaces beside us were filled with hundreds of families. Dad and Kenny went to get food and drinks from the cart vendors who had set up booths along the bank. Mom and I tried to save our place.

Kenny returned: "I've got hot dogs on a stick, candy apples and corn."

Judo classes are taught by a sensei.

A river festival in Japan.

"I like the roasted corn best!" Mom said.

"I'll have a candy apple!" I exclaimed.

Dad appeared: "Have a hot dog or a corn on the cob first, young lady."

I always do what he says when he calls me young lady. We finished eating and drinking our refreshments. Some of the boats had begun to pass by. We asked Mom and Dad if we could watch the fireworks from the bridge. They looked at one another and then agreed. I could tell that they really didn't think this was a good idea.

It was very crowded on the bridge. We managed to get a spot near the edge and the railing. It was really overcrowded. People were pushing and shoving to get in front to see. You had the feeling that they felt their lives depended upon it.

"It's been a long time since I've seen people act so rude. They're almost frantic," Kenny said.

"Try leaning back like this," I said, trying to be helpful. "It's one way to keep from being crushed."

We watched the boat loads of people travelling up and down the river. The lanterns reflected off the water. A huge bonfire was lit and then the fireworks display began. It was very colorful and I enjoyed it.

"I think we should leave early," Dad said. "There are a few million people in this area and we want to try and beat the crowd home."

The bridge was still full of people.

"This is a zoo!" Kenny said.

"Stay in front and just move with this group of people," Dad ordered.

"It isn't like we have a choice!" I yelled.

The subway station was absolutely packed. People with bullhorns were directing the people traffic. We had to line up to get a ticket. It was like the ski lift lines back home. There was lots of pushing and shoving.

"Hey, someone stepped on my foot!"' I yelled.

"Be quiet Lorraine. Everyone is looking at you!" Mom whispered. I felt embarrassed. There it was

again: the old and the new. Again all the rules seemed to have changed for this one night. The normally polite Japanese were in a mood to get home in a hurry. We bought our tickets and lined up in front of a door. We were pushed into the train. At our stop we stood up and were pushed out by the crowd of people coming with us.

When I was in bed later I saw the last of the fireworks exploding over the river and thought of all that we had seen and experienced. Soon it would be time to return to Beaver Creek. I knew that my friends were going to ask me what Japan was like. I started to practice what I would say.

Nihon is a land and a culture that has been changing since the fifteenth century. It is a country of cities.

And yet the countryside is beautiful and relaxing. The music and the arts of *Nihon* are very, very old. They are also very well developed. The Shinkansen is a great symbol of this people who are trying to get to the twenty-first century as fast as they can. Yet, the people carry along the traditions of service, religion and ceremony.

The Japanese are generally extremely polite and gentle. They try to demonstrate respect in all they do.

They are committed to a peaceful existence after a history of war. I have learned a lot but am very tired. *Nihon* is a very busy country. The differences between the United States and Japan are great. And yet there are so many similarities. The land, the resources, the industries, and the recreation activities are very similar. Even the food is very different and yet very much the same.

I always felt off-balance. The crowds always made me feel so small. I now know what high population density is.

Mrs. Sauer will be so proud of me!

Chapter 10

NIHON, SAYONARA

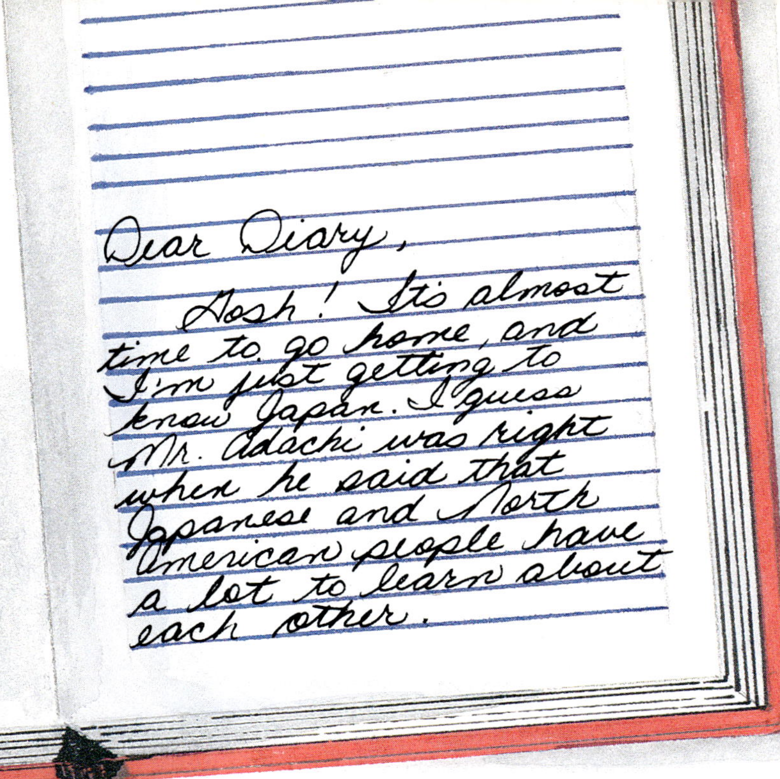

We boarded the express bound for Tokyo. We departed at 9:58 A.M. When we arrived at 12:59 P.M. we had an unusual taxi ride on the way to our hotel. The driver did not know the address! He was very polite and kept apologizing. He then continued to stop other taxi drivers, get new directions and speed along until he needed more directions. I guess that even *Nihonjin* can be confused by the road system in Tokyo.

Mom and I voted to return to the Ginza shopping area for one last round of shopping. Dad said that he would phone the Adachis to join us.

The streets of Ginza had become a pedestrian mall. We enjoyed one last stroll down the strip and some of the side lanes.

Dad and Mr. Adachi were busy talking about Japanese baseball. "The Japanese began playing baseball over one hundred years ago," Mr. Adachi said. "Today it is the biggest spectator sport in Japan, drawing nearly fifteen million fans each year."

"We have two professional leagues called the Pacific League and the Central League," he continued. "In October the champions of each league play a seven game series for the Japanese National Baseball Championship."

"This sounds very much like baseball in North America," Dad said. "We have the American and National Leagues and the two champions play off every October in the World Series. We've always thought of it as the world championship but maybe we should reconsider."

Baseball is very popular in Japan.

"Well," Mr. Adachi said with a chuckle, "sometimes some of the North American teams come over and play exhibition matches against our teams. The scores are usually close."

"However, some of our teams actually have imported American and Canadian players to play for them," he added. "These players are real baseball heroes."

"We have our own Japanese heroes too," Kenny said proudly. "Sadaharu Oh hit 868 home runs for the Yomiuri Giants during his career. That's more home runs than Babe Ruth or Hank Aaron hit in their careers. He now manages the Giants who have won the Central League Championship twenty-four times," he added. "They're just like the New York Yankees."

"You sound like a real fan, Kenny," Dad said.

"I am," Kenny said. "But I'm a fan of the Giants, not the Yankees. My favorite North American team is the Toronto Blue Jays."

Kenny told me about one of the places we had not seen. He said: "Yokohama has a Chinatown. The Japanese really like the food served in the Chinese restaurants."

As we walked back to our hotel from the subway stop, I noticed how hot it was again. We passed a businessman who was wearing a blue pin-striped suit and carrying a fan. He was very well dressed. We also passed a young boy with his school uniform on and I could see the "I ♥ New York" multicolored T-shirt under his white silk shirt.

We sat in the lobby of our hotel and made plans for our departure the next day. Kenny gave me a disk for my computer and said: "This has the files of my trip to the United States on it. Please send me a copy of yours when you have it done."

"I promise I will send you a copy. I'll also write to you. I'm going to try to write a story about the old and new roads of *Nihon*," I said.

Kenny smiled: "Just remember that you and I are living examples of the traditions and future of the United States and Japan."

"But how will you know which road to travel when you come to the fork in the road?" I asked.

"I'll tell you tomorrow," was Kenny's reply.

I fell asleep dreaming of space rockets, computers, robots and huge highrises. Then I was walking through rice fields, sitting in Japanese gardens, and surveying the kingdom from on top of a castle tower. Later, I was a *geisha* performing the *Chado* and then I heard the music of the *shakuhachi*. And always there was the picture of the little girl, the Atom Bomb Dome, the peace tower and a shrine. There was the memory of the wheelchair-bound students touching the memorial monument. My final memory was of the old man who was playing with his little grandson in the park. The old and the new enjoying life.

Mr. and Mrs. Adachi came to drive us to the airport. Mr. Adachi said: "I brought a company van so that we all could travel together."

On the ride out to Narita International Airport everyone was talking except Kenny and me. It was as if we didn't know what to say.

Finally I said: "So what's the answer?"

"I want to have as much of the new as I can without losing what my *ojiisan* taught me," he replied. "I want to have the best of your world and mine!" he continued.

"Can you do that?" I asked.

"I'm going to try!" was Kenny's reply.

"I know that there are many of the traditions of *Nihon* that I will never forget!" I said.

Kenny nodded and simply said, "Keep one eye on the old road and the other on the future!"

I asked Mrs. Adachi what she thought the future of *Nihon* would be like.

She replied: "Well, Lorraine, I think that the *Nihonjin* will continue to visit and trade with the other people throughout the world. We will see more and more original discoveries in the area of technology. *Nihon* will be known for more than copying others' successes. I believe it will become a world leader in communications and electronic technology. Women will also acquire a more equal status in our society. I am sure that we will also face the problems of unemployment and rising costs. We must find ways to house all of our people. Problems will also exist because we are so crowded. But I believe that our commitment to peace and getting along together will allow us to remain a proud people. Our children will be highly educated and will travel more.

"I'm not worried that Kenny will forget the important things of his own culture. The important traditions and customs are what have allowed the *Nihonjin* to go on after each major tragedy. I hope that most of all we will develop more friendships. Your mom and dad, Goro and I, as well as you and Kenny, are very real examples of how our worlds can be different and yet be very close. I will miss you all."

As our plane left the ground of *Nihon* I clutched Kenny's computer disk in my hand. I couldn't wait to get home and begin to input my diary to the data files. I said to Mom: "When I get all of the information sorted into files on the computer I am going to write a report about how the Japanese culture has changed from the times of *Edo* to today."

"You've travelled an old road, a new road and I think you are on a third road that leads to the future. I'm already writing a letter to Mrs. Adachi to begin plans for our next get-together."

"I know what you mean," I whispered and began to write: *It began one day when I noticed a good-looking boy standing in the Bruces' yard . . .*

AND NOW, ON TO THE FUTURE . . .

"Here's my disk with all the information put into categories. I've even begun to write a report. Once the information was all sorted out, the writing seemed easy. I can't believe how much we saw and did when I was in *Nihon*," I told Kenny.

"Well, just remember that if you want more information, write to me or to the Japanese Consulate," replied Kenny.

Mom, Dad and Mr. and Mrs. Adachi were sitting on the beach talking. Mrs. Adachi said: "The culture of the Hawaiian Islands may be the future culture of Japan some day."

"You mean the mixture of people from different backgrounds?" asked Mom.

"That and the amount of Japanese tourism that occurs," replied Mrs. Adachi.

"But we have much more industry, and so many more people. I think that Japan will be more like California than Hawaii," protested Mr. Adachi.

"I am just glad that there are ways of meeting people and making friends in all three places," said Dad.

"Kenny and I think that the future *Nihon* will be very technological, where men and women are more equal, and people are very sincere, respectful and friendly to one another. It will be a country of peace, beauty and happiness. The lessons of the old will always exist because people like Kenny will never forget them. It will have many changes because young people like hamburgers more than they do rice. It will be a place of customs because there is nothing like the grace of the *geisha* or the *Chado* in our world," I said.

"What are the first lines of your story, Lorraine?" asked Mrs. Adachi.

"I have only written two lines to the story. My report on Japan is finished.

"My story is called *TWO ROADS TO JAPAN*. It begins with: *I noticed a good-looking boy standing in the Bruces' yard.* It ends with: *The good-looking boy is no longer a stranger and is now my friend,*" I replied.

Kenny shocked us with a yell: "Surf's up!"

KEY WORDS

Ancestry: The early generations of a family.

Apprentice: A person learning a craft, skill, or trade from a master.

Art, Writing, Music and Meditation: Four skills developed by Japanese nobles as part of their education.

Boarding Pass: A ticket that allows one to go on board a ship, airplane or train.

Buddhist Temple: A building used for Buddhist ceremonies and prayer.

Bullet Train: A popular name for the super fast train in Japan.

Chauvinistic: Having an unreasonable belief in, or attachment to, the superiority of one's own group, gender or place of origin.

Custom: A custom is a tradition or habit. For example, your family may have the custom or tradition of celebrating birthdays.

Customs: The office at a seaport, international airport, or border crossing where imported goods and travel documents are checked.

Effluent: Effluent is waste material, usually pollutant, that is discharged into the environment.

Embargo: A restriction on trade.

Export: The sale and transportation of goods from one country to another.

Face: Dignity, self-respect or prestige.

Feudal: A feudal society has a system of government in which citizens give military and other services to a lord. In return, the lord offers protection and the use of the land he owns.

Food Chain: The way that living things like plants and animals feed and the composition of the environment they live in is linked like a chain. The nourishment of a human population will benefit or suffer depending on the quality of the environment in which members of the food chain (plants and animals) live and grow.

Ginza: Famous commercial street and entertainment area in Tokyo.

Gross National Product: The total value of a nation's goods and services.

Hirohito: Late Emperor of Japan.

Honor: To regard with respect. Individual honor refers to ethics, or principles that one lives by.

Imperial Palace: The home of Japan's Imperial Family, located in Tokyo.

Import: The act of buying and bringing goods into a country.

Industrialization: Development of large, technically advanced industries.

International Date Line: An imaginary line that is agreed upon worldwide as the place where each calendar day begins and ends. It runs north and south through the Pacific Ocean, mostly along the 180th meridian. When it is Sunday just east of the date line, it is Monday just west of it.

International Driver's License: A license that permits a person to operate a motor vehicle in any country in the world.

Losing face: To lose face means to lose dignity in front of others. To have and maintain *face,* or a dignified image, is an important aspect of Japanese culture.

Manufacture: The act of making raw materials into useful items, such as cars.

Mass Transit: A transportation system built to carry large numbers of passengers.

Meditation: Silent reflection on sacred or solemn objects, ideas, values, or principles.

Meiji Era or Meiji Restoration: The Meiji Era refers to a period beginning with the restoration of Emperor Meiji in 1868 and lasting until 1912. During the Meiji Era, Japan was transformed from a feudal nation into a modern one.

Money Exchange: Service outlet for the exchange of foreign currency to local currency.

Monsoon: A wind system that reverses its direction seasonally, thus producing dry and wet seasons.

Patience: The act of remaining calm at all times, especially during periods of suffering or trouble.

Pachinko: A Japanese gambling game which resembles pinball.

Region: The word *region* can refer to either a geographical area (plains, foothills, mountains) or a political division such as a province or state.

Restore: To return something to its former condition.

Rice Cooker: Japanese steam cooker used exclusively for rice.

Rice Paddies: Areas of cultivated ground, generally irrigated, for the planting of fields of rice.

Role: The part one plays in society. You play a role in society as a student and as a son or daughter, brother or sister.

Sexist Characterized by prejudice or discrimination on the basis of sex.

Shinto Shrine: A religious structure at which Shinto deities and ancestors are worshiped.

Stocks: Stocks are units of ownership in a particular company. Companies sell stocks, or shares, to raise money.

Terraced: Built on several levels that slope upwards.

Time Zones: Geographical regions in which the same standard of time is used. The world is divided into twenty-four time zones.

Tradition: Customs or actions characteristic of a country or people. Ceremonies that have been practiced for some time are traditions.

Travellers' Checks: Checks that can be used in place of cash. Travellers use them because they can not be cashed if stolen.

Typhoon: A violent tropical hurricane that forms over the western Pacific.

Value: To regard highly.

Voucher: A receipt that shows that something has been paid for.

INDEX

PHOTOCREDITS

Albert, Rolf - 15 inset, 19, 22 bottom, 32, 42 bottom, 44, 50 left, 54, 55, 56, 68, 78, 90, 95 inset, 100, 107.

Chatelin Features, by Toshi Chatelin - 29 left, 42 top, 47 left, 52 left and right.

Hokkaido Government Tourist Bureau - 63.

INTEX Osaka - 94 and 94 inset.

JNTO (Japan National Tourist Organization) - 39, 47 right.

Ministry of Foreign Affairs, Japan - 40, 60, 61, 62, 66 left, 93, 103.

Ministry of Tourist Information - 38, 43, 48 left, 63, 77 bottom.

New York Times Company - 83, © 1941, Reprint by permission.

Omotani, Les - 29 right, 67, 73 top right and bottom, 75, 77 top left and right, 81, 86 left and right, 87, 88 left and right, 89 inset, 97 top left, 98 left and right.

The I.S.E.I, (International Society for Educational Information), Tokyo Inc. - 20, top four food pictures.